SpringerBriefs in Political Science

For further volumes:
http://www.springer.com/series/8871

Donald H. Taylor, Jr.

Balancing the Budget is a Progressive Priority

Donald H. Taylor, Jr.
Sanford School of Public Policy
Duke University
502 Science Drive
Durham, North Carolina
USA

ISSN 2191-5466   e-ISSN 2191-5474
ISBN 978-1-4614-3663-8   e-ISBN 978-1-4614-3664-5
DOI 10.1007/978-1-4614-3664-5
Springer New York Dordrecht Heidelberg London

Library of Congress Control Number: 2012935690

© Springer Science+Business Media, LLC 2012
All rights reserved. This work may not be translated or copied in whole or in part without the written permission of the publisher (Springer Science+Business Media, LLC, 233 Spring Street, New York, NY 10013, USA), except for brief excerpts in connection with reviews or scholarly analysis. Use in connection with any form of information storage and retrieval, electronic adaptation, computer software, or by similar or dissimilar methodology now known or hereafter developed is forbidden.
The use in this publication of trade names, trademarks, service marks, and similar terms, even if they are not identified as such, is not to be taken as an expression of opinion as to whether or not they are subject to proprietary rights.

Printed on acid-free paper

Springer is part of Springer Science+Business Media (www.springer.com)

Prologue

The first edition of this book was self-published via Kindle Direct publishing in the midst of the debt ceiling debate in August 2011; I am glad for the opportunity to publish a revised version that takes account of the work of the so-called Super Committee, and which tries to place to the ongoing struggle to develop a plan for a long-range sustainable budget in the overall context of the 2012 election and beyond.

The primary facts have not changed from New Year's Day 2011 to late April 2012. The main task before the government of the United States in 2011 was to enact policies that could improve the economic situation of the country (economic growth and job creation), while credibly addressing our long-range budget deficit problem that will some day produce a debt crisis if it goes unaddressed. We failed on both accounts.

That remains the primary task of the government of the United States in 2012.

We do not now have a debt crisis. A debt crisis would begin when investors are unwilling to loan us more money because they are afraid we will not pay them back. If so, we will have to pay a higher interest rate to tempt investors, diverting more money from productive uses to service our debt. Austere and immediate budget cuts to programs like Medicare and Social Security would likely follow. However, the United States did not experience a debt crisis during 2011. There are many investors willing to loan the US government money at extremely low interest rates, but this situation will not last forever without changes.

The country did experience a political crisis in late Summer 2011 over the raising of the debt ceiling that was manufactured by Congressional Republicans for political leverage. Since World War II, the debt ceiling has been raised dozens of times, and since the debt ceiling is denominated in nominal dollars, it will have to be raised continuously in the foreseeable future regardless of what policies we enact, or what political party is in power. However, these debates will never again be the same.

The decision by Standard & Poor's to downgrade the long-term US debt to AA+ from AAA status was triggered by the political theater witnessed as well as the policy "no man's land" into which we remain in January 2012. For all the bluster about the deficit, the debt ceiling deal did not address the primary drivers of our long-term problem: a tax code that cannot raise the revenue necessary to pay for any plausible level of overall spending, and a plan to address health care costs that we will actually try.

The locus of political action during the Fall of 2011 was the 12-member Super Committee created as part of the debt ceiling deal. In fact, once this group was created, it assured that virtually nothing else would happen in Congress during the Fall of 2011. This group of six Democrats and six Republicans could have specified alternate cuts in excess of $1.5 trillion over the next decade, or an even larger plan, to replace automatic cuts to Medicare and Defense spending that were designed to maximize the chance of a deal, but none was agreed to.

December 2011 saw a deal to extend the payroll tax cut passed through February 2012, with the extension now passed for the balance of 2012. We can afford larger deficits in the short run given how cheaply we can borrow money, we just need to couple such actions with long-term plans to address our underlying fiscal problems.

In short, we need to be able to walk and chew gum at the same time, but we appear to have been unable to do either for the past year, and there is no reason for optimism that this will change soon.

As we head into the 2012 election, the task remains the same: we need to undertake policies to improve our economy in the short run, while seeking a long-run plan to move slowly toward a balanced budget in the future. To achieve the latter will require some profound reform of our health care system and an increase in the proportion of the economy collected in taxes. There are other issues to be gotten straight, but without addressing those two realities (taxes are too low given any plausible level of federal spending and projected health care costs too high absent reform) we will never again have anything near a balanced budget.

This book offers a policy-driven way out of the box, while making the case that Progressives have more to lose than do Conservatives by delaying action.

Preface

The last two federal elections have heralded the rise of two seemingly opposing political movements. In 2008, Barack Obama invigorated and mobilized young voters and raised enormous amounts of campaign money online. This helped propel him to the first victory by a Democratic candidate in two generations in places like North Carolina and Virginia. The 2010 election saw the rise of the Tea Party, expressing discontent with incumbents, and their view that elected officials were overstepping the Constitutionally described bounds of their power, fueling a Republican resurgence just 2 years after they were written off as a governing force. In both cases, people who had not been involved in politics became vitally engaged.

The common theme that links these otherwise disparate movements was what they both said they most wanted: change.

The euphoria of 2008 among Obama supporters was short-lived. The limitless hopes for reform, changing the tone in Washington, and addressing the big issues in a cerebral manner seemed a quaint memory on election night November 2010. While many interpret the Republican resurgence in the 2010 election as a repudiation of President Obama and his too-liberal policies, some on the left flank of the Democratic party wanted a primary challenge of the President because they view him as having abandoned them. Of course the reality of the economic crisis, which helped to pave the way for President Obama's election, also provided the fire for the election campaign of 2010, and will be the President's biggest reelection roadblock.

A cataclysmic 2010 election for the Democratic party gave way to the *lame duck* session of the 111th Congress that produced a flurry of legislation, most consequentially for the fiscal state of our nation an extension of the tax rates that were set to revert to 2001 levels on January 1, 2011, and a payroll tax holiday of two percentage points for workers that would pump more money into the economy than did the American Reinvestment and Recovery Act of 2008 (aka the stimulus). By Christmas 2010, Obama, who was written off at Thanksgiving as a one-term President, was said to be back and ready to govern from a more centrist position. The pace of change in political momentum is dizzying.

The reality of divided government has been difficult, as evidenced by "tooth-and-nail" fights over continuing budget resolutions for 2011 and the debt ceiling debate that sucked all the oxygen out of the "policy room" for the Summer of 2011, even as the economy languished and further governmental intervention seemed warranted yet politically impossible. The Super Committee created by the debt ceiling agreement captured most of the attention of official Washington during the Fall of 2011, yet in the end failed to reach an agreement that would replace the $1.2 trillion in automatic cuts to Medicare and Defense spending over the next decade agreed to as a default, much less an elusive Grand Bargain.

As 2011 ended, an extension of the payroll tax reduction from 6.2% to 4.2% for 2012 was agreed upon through February 2012, but has now been extended for the entire year.

The rapid swings in the mood of the electorate—from euphoria to stupor and back again—demonstrate the restless state of our nation. We have been at war for 10 years in a conflict that is both the longest in our nation's history, but also one in which most citizens haven't been asked to sacrifice for, or contribute to, directly. The economy boomed in the 1990s, stagnated in the middle part of the last decade, and nearly collapsed into a depression in 2008–2009. A recovery has now begun, but it is slow and many Millions remain out of work. In a decade, the primary conversation in our nation changed from how to spend the peace dividend (the federal budget surplus!) as President Bush was inaugurated, to whether our economy can create jobs, move back into consistent and robust growth as an expectation, and reduce the very large deficits that have occurred due to the economic downturn, and take on our structural budget problems.

Through all of these ups and downs, one thing has remained abundantly clear: it is easier to achieve a political victory by emphasizing that you are not as bad as the "other side" than it is to address the most profound problems facing our nation.

The Big Questions

There are many consequential questions facing our nation: the proper role of government in our lives; the appropriate level of taxation as well as the fairness and efficiency of how the tax burden is shared. The twin issues of access to and cost of health care. What size military do we need, and when should we use it? How will we care appropriately for the elderly, both the happily retired and the infirm, as the baby boomers move into eligibility for Medicare and Social Security? How do we practically interpret the Constitution to guide how we address all of these issues?

These questions all collide in one place: the federal budget of the United States.

Our nation faces a long-term budget crisis that will manifest itself through ongoing and predictably large deficits—the spending of more money than is collected in taxes in a given year—and the ongoing accumulation of debt as each annual deficit is added to our cumulative national debt. The US has had only four balanced budgets since I have been alive (1969, 1998–2000), but the looming problem is more severe, and there is increasing recognition that something must be done. But what?

This long-term budget crisis is first and foremost a health care cost problem that is exacerbated by the retirement of the baby boom generation. Social Security faces a purely demographic problem (fewer workers paying taxes per retiree), while Medicare shares the same demographic problem, but joins it with our nation's seemingly insatiable ability to consume health care, even as 51 million of us have no health insurance. The cost of health care has gone up much faster than overall inflation for the past 40 years, with similar rates of increase for government and private insurers. The entire health care system has a cost problem, but it manifests itself most clearly in the federal budget via Medicare (insurance for the elderly) and Medicaid (insurance for the poor).

It is the claim of this book that Progressives have more at stake in developing a long-range balanced budget than do Conservatives precisely because we believe that government has a positive role to play in modern life. If we do not develop a path to a sustainable federal budget, there will be no room left for government to invest in new opportunities that could make people and our country better off. And if we wait to address the budget deficit problem only after a debt-driven crisis, there will be fewer options available, which will endanger programs that are so important to Progressives, namely Medicare, Medicaid, and Social Security.

It is the thesis of this book that slowing the rate of health care cost inflation is a necessary, but not a sufficient, condition to achieving a balanced budget at some point in the long term (20–30 years). The passage of the Affordable Care Act was a positive step, but more are needed. If we can successfully address our health care cost problem, then we have a chance to achieve a balanced budget if we get some other policy options right. However, if we don't address our health care cost problem, then we have no chance of achieving a balanced budget regardless of what else we do because health care costs are such a central driver of our long-term deficit. Anyone claiming to want a long-range sustainable budget needs a credible health reform strategy to address the interrelated problems of cost, coverage, and quality.

While health care has a tremendous budgetary impact, it is different from other issues affecting the budget because success means that we will either provide less care and/or pay providers less for care than what we will do by default. This will be very hard, as there is ample evidence that our culture has more trouble making tradeoffs about health care than other budgetary items. It is far more complicated for Medicare to purchase health care for the elderly than it is for Social Security to mail checks. This book provides a subtle, nuanced perspective that frames health policy as the most pressing long-term budgetary issue, while bringing expertise in health policy to bear in a way that does not oversimplify health reform.

It is a premise of this book that we will deal with the deficit at some point, the only question is when and under what circumstances? Can we act in a reasoned manner to face up to our challenges in a bipartisan manner? Or will it take an economic calamity of unknown trigger, timing, and content to force us to act?

It would be much better for us to be proactive, and this book is my vision for the way forward in achieving this goal.

Book Outline

The outline of the book is as follows. Chapter 1 outlines a progressive vision for why and how to achieve a long-term sustainable federal budget by placing the main topics in context: health care, Social Security, military spending, and developing a tax code that pays for the spending we say we want and does so in a manner that encourages economic growth and job creation.

Chapter 2 briefly describes why the budget deficit and the cumulative debt of our nation are problems, and why the levels of cumulative debt we have and are likely to incur over the next decade will lead to problems for our country without policy changes.

Chapters 3–7 focus in detail on health reform because health care costs are the primary driver of the deficit and a clear understanding of the issues are needed to make good policy. These chapters outline the historical roots of our health care cost problem, identify what the Affordable Care Act did and did not do, and discuss the politics of health reform and how the way our culture views death and the limits of medicine enable the politics of health reform to be so powerful. Finally, Chap. 7 provides a way forward in health reform that has at its center the belief that we must develop a bipartisan health reform strategy in which both political parties can get some credit, but also have some responsibility for what will be a 20–30-year effort to develop a sustainable health care system.

Chapter 8 focuses on Social Security, a key program that serves as the bedrock of the social safety net. I advocate undertaking long-term reforms now even though planned benefits can be paid for the next quarter century, in large part because doing so sooner rather than later will enable Progressive to drive changes to the program on their terms, and most importantly, so the program can be fixed and "taken off the table" allowing us to focus on health care costs.

Chapter 9 provides brief thoughts on Defense spending, while Chap. 10 focuses on what proportion of the economy should be redistributed by government. The debate over a balanced budget amendment focuses on this question; however, an evidence-based discussion of this topic must make clear what level of taxation will be required, and what spending will be possible at different balance points. In short, the public wants low taxes and high spending, and we cannot continue to have both. Chapter 11 provides a direction for reforming the tax code in a way that increases the tax revenue flowing into the federal government while taking several steps to improve our economy and to incentivize job creation.

Chapter 12 provides concluding thoughts on our need to move ahead with a long-term plan to balance the budget.

Note: Figures, tables, references, and supplementary material for the book can be found at http://sites.duke.edu/donaldhtaylorjr/balancing-the-budget-is-a-progressive-priority/.

Durham, NC, USA   Donald H. Taylor, Jr.

Acknowledgments

Many people have assisted me in writing this book, but several warrant special mention. Khuwailah Beyah helped with the many details required to pull it together. Kyle Hudson read the entire manuscript over a weekend late in the game. My co-bloggers at The Incidental Economist, Austin Frakt and Aaron Carroll, helped me to think through many of the issues in the book by reading their excellent work. They are the best health policy bloggers around. Austin also read several chapters and commented. Marc Bellemare read several chapters and talked with me about the themes of the book over the past year, as did David Schanzer who also provided insight into the workings of Congress during the health reform debate that proved very insightful. Tyler Cowen gave me some advice about the use of Kindle Direct Publishing, and Katie Rosman answered my questions about the book industry at several points in the process, as did John Covell, who also read several chapters and discussed them with me.

Others who read chapters and/or discussed the themes of the book with me are: Minda Brooks, Frank Hill, Mike Munger, Mac McCorkle, and my dad Hugh Taylor.

I am grateful to Jon Gurstelle, Senior Editor for Economics and Political Science at Springer for publishing this second edition.

All errors or omissions are my responsibility.

Durham, NC, USA   Donald H. Taylor, Jr.
                                                                                 www.donaldhtaylorjr.com

Contents

1 **Progressives Need a Balanced Budget** 1
   Why a Balanced Budget Is a Progressive Priority 2
   What Proportion of the Economy Should Be Redistributed
   by Government? 4
   The Standard: The Ins Match the Outs 5
      The Redistribution Rabbit Trail 6
   Multiple Plans, Same Diagnosis 6
   Social Security, Defense, and Taxes 7
   The Challenge 8

2 **Why the Deficit Is a Problem** 9
   How Big Is Too Big? 10
   The Mere Existence of a Deficit Is Not Evidence of a Problem 11
   The Kitchen Table 11
   Fast Forward to 2020 12
   Deficits Crowd Out Progressive Priorities 14
   Not If, but When? 14

3 **Health Reform: The Problems** 17
   The Problems 21
      Problem Number 1: Cost 21
      Big Problem Number 2: Lack of Coverage 24
      Big Problem Number 3: Quality 28

4 **Health Reform: The Policy** 31
   First Step, or Last? 32
      Individual Mandate 33
      Insurance Reform to Ban Denial of Coverage
      for Preexisting Conditions 34
      Setting Up State-Based Insurance Markets 35
      Medicaid Expansions 36

	Cut Planned Medicare Spending to Partially Finance Insurance Expansions..	37
	Increase Taxes to Partially Expand Insurance Expansions	38
	Aspects of ACA That Could Address Health Care Cost Inflation..	38
	Tax on High Cost Insurance	38
	The Independent Payment Advisory Board	39
	Medicare Innovation Center, Etc.	41
5	**Health Reform: The Politics**..	**43**
	Political Flashpoints: Individual Mandate and Rationing........................	45
	The Patients' Choice Act	46
	Soft Individual Mandates	46
	End Tax Exclusion of Employer Paid Insurance...............................	47
	Tax Credit Would Provide Catastrophic Coverage Only	47
	Proposed Board of Experts to Make Policy Decisions for the Entire Health Care System	48
	Cake Not Fully Cooked..	48
	The Political Bottom Line...	49
6	**Health Reform: The Barriers**..	**51**
	We Have to Develop Our Own System...	52
	The Biggest Obstacle Is Us...	52
	Can Anyone Say No?...	53
	Saying No to Palliative Care	55
	Focus on Value	57
	How Do We Start?	58
7	**Health Reform: Next Steps**...	**59**
	Overview of Suggested Reforms	60
	Replace the Individual Mandate with Catastrophic Coverage................	60
	Cost Reduction...	62
	Settle Coverage Questions and Focus on Costs	63
	Reform the Tax Preference of Employer Paid Health Insurance	63
	Move to End the Medicaid Program Over the Next Decade	64
	Expand Medicare's Ability to Be an Active Purchaser...........................	67
	Expand the Authority of the Independent Payment Advisory Board..	68
	Give the Kitchen Sink Approach to Improving Quality and Reducing Costs a Chance to Work...	68
	Experimentation with Competitive Bidding	69
	Medical Malpractice Reform	72
	Cap Federal Health Spending Backstopped by a Tax-Based Fail Safe	74
	I Do Not Favor Raising the Medicare Age.......................................	74
	The Way Forward..	75

8	**Social Security**	77
	Principles for Social Security Reform	78
	The Nature of the Problem	78
	What About Life Expectancy Gains?	80
	Specific Social Security Reforms	81
	Expand the Safety Net by Enhancing Low Income Earner's Benefits on the Basis of Years Worked	81
	Increase the Amount to Which the Social Security Payroll Tax Is Applied	81
	Reduce Initial Benefits for Higher Income Persons	82
	Change How Benefits Are Calculated and Updated for All Beneficiaries	82
	Do Not Raise the Full Retirement Age	83
	Payroll Tax Cut	83
	The Way Forward	84
9	**Guns vs. Medicare**	85
	Military Spending in Context	86
	Cross-National Military Spending	86
	Fiscal Commission Recommendations	87
10	**How Much Should Government Spend?**	89
	Can the Public Decide?	90
	The Public Finds Health Care Choices Harder	91
	Setting a Target for Balance	92
11	**Tax Reform**	95
	Mix of Federal Taxes Over Time	96
	Key Goals of Tax Code	96
	Fiscal Commission Tax Reform	97
	Income Tax Rates	98
	End the Corporate Income Tax	99
	Inheritance Tax	102
	Other Tax Changes I Have Proposed	102
12	**What Will It Take for Us to Act?**	103
	Politics of the Past Year	104
	Policy Consensus of the Past Year	105
	Big Events in 2012	106
	Hold Hands and Jump	107

Chapter 1
Progressives Need a Balanced Budget

Progressives need a balanced federal budget more than Conservatives, both to provide room for new government action when needed as well as to protect the key programs of Medicare, Medicaid, and Social Security. For this reason, developing a long-term plan to balance the federal budget should be at the top of the Progressive agenda, because without doing so, the ability to address Progressive priorities via government action will be rendered moot.

Conservatives talk at length about fiscal responsibility and lament "tax and spend." However, when in power they have practiced "don't tax, yet still spend." When viewing the inevitable deficits, they claim they prove that government doesn't work and advocate more tax cuts. Because Progressives believe government does have a key role in modern society, we must lead the charge to develop a sustainable federal budget that leaves room for government intervention to address important problems both now and in the future, while protecting Progressive priorities such as Medicare and Social Security.

Progressives also have blind spots. The current federal budget is unsustainable. This means that we cannot keep doing what we are now doing in the way of taxes and spending without the routine use of deficit financing to pay for programs that are ongoing and predictable—namely retirement and health care costs via Social Security, Medicare, Medicaid, and large military expenditures. If we develop a plan for a balanced budget, it will require hard decisions that cannot simply be a defense of current programmatic funding levels of key programs, cutting military spending, and an increase in taxes. The overall math of a long-term balanced budget is fairly clear: current spending levels will have to fall, and taxes will have to rise, but there are many important decisions to be made about how we get there.

Neither the intervention by the federal government in response to the financial crisis via the Toxic Asset Relief Program (TARP), nor the American Reinvestment and Recovery Act (ARRA, aka the stimulus) has made the federal budget unsustainable. Deficits will always be incurred during times of emergency. It is the inability to pay for predictable expenditures over the next several decades given our tax code and spending obligations that make the federal budget unsustainable.

It is preferable to make the hard decisions needed to develop a plan for a long-term balanced budget before a debt-driven financial crisis (no one willing to lend us money at low rates; we do not have this problem now) forces us to act, at which time there will be fewer options, placing key programs such as Medicare and Social Security at risk. And it is unclear who will wield the balance of political power when a future debt-driven crisis could force quick action.

Progressives can best represent their vision of how a long-term balanced budget should be achieved by driving the agenda.

Why a Balanced Budget Is a Progressive Priority

The current unsustainable path of the federal budget makes new federal spending on issues such as education, energy, and the environment very difficult. For example, the Race to the Top initiatives have been heralded as having a positive impact on education improvement across the nation. At $4.35 billion , the cost of the program is quite small in the context of the federal government (FY 2011 budget over $3.5 trillion), but nevertheless may be consequential in stimulating positive changes. However, annual deficits larger than $1 trillion make it difficult for us to consider new spending, even if it is a relatively small amount.

And in a real sense, this intuition that we cannot afford to spend more without a clear plan to address large annual deficits is correct. We cannot and should not achieve a balanced budget overnight, but we do need to get our fiscal house in order and determine the amount of spending that is desired and then raise the amount of revenue needed to finance this spending. The absence of a plan to address the deficit over the long-run crowds out investment in the short run and puts current programs at risk down the road. Similarly, any attempts to address the continuing mortgage and housing crisis or develop a federal jobs bill are likely rendered politically moot without a comprehensive, long-range plan to address our fiscal imbalance.

It is unclear how close President Obama and Speaker Boehner may have really been to a "grand bargain" on a long-term deficit plan during the debt ceiling debate. Even less clear is whether the two leaders could have brought their respective Political Party's along on such a large-scale deal in such a short period of time. While many are skeptical of the ability of any real change to take place during an election year, the campaign provides a chance for the President and Progressives to educate the public and make clear that we do need a comprehensive long-range plan to balance the budget. It is possible that momentum toward this task may be the only way to politically enable needed short-term efforts to expand jobs and support our economy. If the "grand bargain" had passed in August 2011, then maybe we would have moved to address the jobs crisis more forcefully the next week.

If we do not develop a long-term plan for a balanced budget, not only will we likely be politically unable to address our immediate needs to bolster the economy, but by 2020 there will be no money left to do anything other than pay for Social Security, federal health care expenditures (Medicare, Medicaid, exchange subsidies), the military and interest on the debt given our current system of taxation. Under this status quo that includes a politically imaginable extension of the current tax rates, we will be unable to move ahead on initiatives in areas like education, green technology, infrastructure, or the environment.

If Progressives would commit to a sustainable federal budget and paint a picture of priorities in how to get there we would do two things.

First, directly engage a crucial problem facing our nation. The most important reason to do it is because it is the right thing to do.

Second, we would call the bluff of Conservatives, who seem to only care about deficits when in opposition, and never when discussing tax cuts. Our disinterest in this topic has allowed Conservatives to get away with rank hypocrisy in the area of fiscal responsibility because the public has, perhaps rightly, seen us as mostly interested in developing new programs. If Progressives provide leadership in this important and difficult area, Conservatives will be forced to respond (and some want to do so), and the reality of the situation is that spending will have to fall and taxes will have to rise if we are to achieve a sustainable budget.

This book will make the case for how I think we should balance the budget over the long run, with the key being the next steps on health care reform, since health care costs are the nation's biggest long term fiscal problem. Medicare and the health care system generally require profound changes. Social Security needs to be tweaked, and can be done in ways that expand the safety net nature of the program if we move sooner rather than later to reform the program. Defense spending must decline in a thoughtful manner. And tax receipts will have to rise to pay for the spending we say we want if we are ever going to have a balanced budget again. We need a growing and prosperous economy to support the spending we believe is optimal, so reform of the tax code with economic growth and job creation as a central goal is paramount.

Some Progressives shrink from this conversation due to fear that engaging in it will endanger programs and spending that we believe to be crucial. The truth is the opposite. Not engaging in this conversation likely puts such crucial programs in more jeopardy, because waiting for a debt-driven financial crisis to address our long-term deficit problem will likely mean there are far fewer choices and options available, and large spending cuts to Medicare, Medicaid, and Social Security would ensue. The longer we wait to start, the fewer options we will have, so we need to engage the discussion now, in a way that allows us to make our case.

Making the federal budget sustainable over the long term will be very difficult due to the degree to which public opinion is frankly delusional: we want low taxes and high spending. Providing a detailed vision for balancing the budget is politically risky. While the outline of the final deal may be straightforward in policy terms, it is not clear what the first step is, and everyone is afraid to make it mistakenly. And both political parties have experienced recent electoral success by essentially arguing "we are not as bad as they are!" which is what I would assert was the primary message of the last three elections (2006, 2008, and 2010). With an external threat like World War II, our nation was driven together by common enemies. Developing a sustainable budget is far more likely to put us at war with one another.

What Proportion of the Economy Should Be Redistributed by Government?

Conservatives have correctly identified a key question we must address as a nation: what proportion of our economy will be redistributed by the federal government? However, they have done so as a foil to argue for lower taxes, but have not identified the spending cuts required for a balanced budget given our current tax code, much less one that brings in even less revenue as a percent of GDP.

Answering this question and following through with policy choices to implement it is required if we are going to develop a sustainable federal budget. In that sense it is a very practical question. However, there are ways in which addressing this hard question as a nation will have profound intangible benefits. If we manage to have a serious, fact-based conversation, with debate, disagreement, give and take, and eventually a consensus agreement, that would be good for our nation. If we succeed, it will mean that we have done something hard together, and in doing so will have helped to define in a practical manner the rights and responsibilities of being an American in the twenty-first century. By rights and responsibilities, I mean what you can expect to receive, and what you are expected to provide.

In 2011, Republicans in the Senate offered a balanced budget amendment to the Constitution that would cap federal spending at 18% of the GDP and require a two-thirds supermajority in Congress to raise taxes. The House Republicans passed a Cut, Cap, and Balance proposal during the Summer of 2011 that also set the target for achieving balance at 18% of GDP. This would require a balanced budget at the historical average level of taxation seen in the past 40 years, which is obviously mathematically possible, but practically improbable because Republicans lack a credible health reform plan that could achieve the savings needed to achieve long-term balance at 18% of GDP. In fact, when in arguing against the Affordable Care Act (ACA) during the last election, many Republicans pledged to "not cut a dime from Medicare." Capping federal spending at 18% of the GDP, while pledging to not cut Medicare spending, is a nonsensical position. It is like saying I will eat potato chips on my couch all winter and in the summer look great in my bathing suit.

The President's Fiscal Responsibility Commission report (hereafter The Fiscal Commission) set a target of 21% of GDP as the point at which balance should be achieved, around the year 2035, which is a more plausible level of spending and taxes at which to seek balance. Achieving long-term balance at 21% of GDP will still require profound health reform beyond that passed in the ACA, and the policies suggested in this book are made with an aim toward long term balance at 21% of GDP.

Progressives have tended to focus on the importance of spending programs, and the negative effect on people's lives if spending is cut, and we are quick to suggest raising taxes to close the deficit gap. However, we must take care to develop a long-term plan for balance that ensures a robust economy. The last balanced budget came in the year 2000 that saw tax receipts as a proportion of GDP at 20.6%, the largest amount received in taxes in 50 years. The more you believe in the importance of federal spending programs, the more you need predictable revenues, which means you need a robust and growing economy. And the last decade has shown that at least as far as job growth goes, there is a big problem with the US economy. Simply focusing efforts on maintaining spending levels of current programs will not be enough. We must develop a plan for a long-range balanced budget that does all that we can to incentivize economic growth and job creation while creating a tax system that can collect the money needed to pay for the spending we desire.

The Standard: The Ins Match the Outs

We need a long-range plan for a balanced budget, in which all of the ins match all of the outs. The ins of course are taxes, while the outs are expenditures, be they explicit flow of funds toward programs such as Medicare, the military, NIH, or through aspects of the tax code that favor one type of behavior over another (a so-called tax expenditure), like the Earned Income Tax Credit (EITC). The EITC allows families with some income, but below the level at which they pay federal income taxes, to receive money from the federal government in what amounts to a negative income tax. It is a very efficient way to provide money to lower income persons if that is your policy goal. The total cost to the treasury of the EITC was around $48 billion last year, all of which flowed to persons with relatively low income. Thus, if the EITC did not exist, the deficit would have been around $48 billion smaller last year. There are thousands of such tax expenditures (most smaller, but some larger) in the federal tax code, that all told increased the deficit by around $1.1 trillion last year.

Eliminating all tax expenditures would nearly balance the federal budget next year, with no change in tax rates. You may be nodding your head and saying, "let's do it, who knew it could be so easy!" I suspect many who are for ending tax expenditures in the abstract will change their tune when they realize that the largest tax expenditures benefit middle and upper income earners, notably the ability to deduct mortgage interest from taxable income (cost around $104 billion in 2010), or the tax free income that employees receive when their employer pays for a portion of their health insurance (cost $106 billion in 2010; $250 billion when summing all the related tax expenditures associated with the tax preference given to employer provided health insurance). It is very common in talks I give on health reform and the budget deficit to find out that those who are "fed up with all this spending" actually quite like most of it, because most people at such events are upper middle-class folks who receive most of the benefits of tax expenditures. We hate spending only in the abstract, while vastly over estimating the size of programs we dislike, and underestimating the cost of ones we do like.

The key is that the debate cannot be abstract, but must be practical. Most Americans seem to want low taxes and high spending. However, when you begin to enumerate the types of spending that could be cut, they are loath to touch the biggest items: Social Security, Medicare, military spending. In the abstract, most are in favor of a balanced budget. It is less clear that we can marshal the courage to enact the practical (and hard) choices to actually achieve one. The only way to have a meaningful discussion is to focus on both the taxes necessary to achieve balance at a given spending level (I think 21% of GDP is feasible), and the programmatic spending that would be feasible at that level. This means that the discussion could be iterative, with initial targets being altered in either direction. This is fine, but we need to start.

The Redistribution Rabbit Trail

A common Conservative talking point is that they do not object to government spending, they simply object to redistribution of income via government spending. This is a nonsensical position, even if it appears to be an effective applause line at a political rally. Every government program redistributes income. For one to not do so would mean there is some tax that is collected and returned to citizens in the exact same proportion that the tax was collected. Medicare, Social Security, military spending, highway funding, the tax deductibility of home mortgage interest, the EITC, and every other program and tax expenditure in the tax code are redistributive. If you think home mortgage interest deduction is not redistributive, then no one should be opposed to ending this aspect of the tax code. The real debate is what type of redistribution we will have. And then deciding we will pay for it.

Multiple Plans, Same Diagnosis

Even with a normal economy, changes must be made or the normal functioning of the federal budget (default taxes and spending) as it now exists will lead to predictably large deficits and cumulative levels of debt that will harm our economy. Groups like the Peterson Foundation and the Concord Coalition have long been touting the issues of balanced budgets and fiscal responsibility, but the latter part of 2010 and 2011 saw many groups engage in this discussion and provide their vision of how a balanced budget should be achieved. The Committee for a Responsible Federal Budget has identified 32 such plans from across the ideological spectrum. The plans differ in the target proportion of GDP at which to balance the budget, the timing to achieve balance (what year), the recommendations made regarding spending priorities, and how the tax code might be altered in terms of what types of taxes are used to collect the revenue necessary to fund the federal government. However, they all identify one overriding problem that makes our current federal budget unsustainable: health care costs.

Put another way, if we don't address health care costs, there is no feasible way that we can achieve a balanced and sustainable balanced budget. If we do address health care costs, then we have a chance to develop a sustainable budget if we get some other questions correct.

What do we actually need to achieve in the way of health care costs? The US now spends around $8,500 per capita on health care. Tracking spending over time is most meaningfully done via per capita spending, because that ties the actual resources we put toward health care delivery to the size of the population. We do not need to spend less than $8,500 per capita on health care. What we need to do is slow the rate of inflation or increase in what we spend on a per capita basis. I call this a cut because it is a decrease in what we are expected to spend, by default. And it will be hard because health care costs have gone up so steadily in the past few decades, in large part because Americans like to consume health care.

At historical health care inflation rates, we would be expected to spend about $14,000 per capita in 2020. Spending just $13,500 per capita in 2020 would be an achievement, and spending $12,000 per capita in 2020 would be a miracle. Anything less than the projected spending level per capita is best understood as a cut because it is less than what we will spend by default. We have got to slow the rate of cost inflation in health care, if we are going to develop a balanced budget. If we got to the point where health care spending per capita grew only 1 percentage point faster than the GDP over the long run, it would be the greatest public policy achievement in the history of the United States. That is the goal I set later in the book, along with some of the policy ideas to get there. It will be hard to achieve, but I don't think we have a choice but to try.

Social Security, Defense, and Taxes

Social Security has real financing problems that must be fixed. However, the magnitude of the problem facing Social Security is much less severe than that facing Medicare. This is because Social Security only faces the demographic problem presented by the baby boomers moving into eligibility for the program, namely that there are fewer persons paying payroll taxes per beneficiary as compared to the past. Since Social Security's benefits are cash indexed to inflation in one way or another, a fairly straightforward, and predictable solution can be found. Medicare, on the other hand, joins the same demographic problem with the fact that it purchases health care, including innovations tomorrow that are unknown today, a far more complex undertaking than is the mailing of checks.

There are a variety of fixes that could make Social Security solvent for the rest of this century. They include increasing taxes or decreasing benefits, or of course a mixture. I make the case for my preferred tweaking of the Social Security program, but what we most need is to pick one fix quickly, move ahead, and then focus our greatest attention on slowing the rate of health care cost inflation. One worry is that we will spend inordinate time debating Social Security and use a great deal of political bandwidth and capital to fix what is really a fairly straightforward problem. If this debate keeps us from engaging the health care cost debate, that will be very bad. On the other hand, since a Social Security fix is simpler, addressing that first and taking it off the table would allow us to focus policy energy on addressing health care costs. This is my preferred approach.

In any event, inaction on both Social Security and Medicare is a recipe for disaster from a Progressive point of view because it puts us on a path to only addressing the deficit after a debt-driven crisis that will put Medicare and Social Security at more risk than will an open discussion of these programs now.

I view military spending as linked to health care spending. There is no obvious connection between the two, other than the fact that they are both very large parts of our federal budget (military spending accounted for 20% of federal spending in 2010; Medicare and Medicaid together accounted for 21% in 2010, and Medicare alone will account for 20% in 2020 under current growth scenarios). They also happen to be the two parts of our budget that are most exceptional in terms of international comparisons. I do believe we have to cut defense spending, but do not propose a detailed strategy for this because it is not my policy expertise. As a citizen, of course, I do state some preferences. In the end, the old tradeoff taught in high school civics class "guns vs. butter" is actually "guns vs. Medicare." What you are willing to do in the way of cutting one defines how much you must cut the other if we are to achieve a sustainable budget. If you believe we cannot cut military spending appreciably, then you must *really* be for Medicare cuts, and vice versa.

Finally, we need a tax code that can pay for the spending that we say we want. However, we must reform our tax code to provide the maximum possible incentive for job creation and economic growth possible while raising the needed revenue. Progressives need a robust and growing economy to fund the level of governmental spending that we believe is needed. I lay out a general tax reform framework that modifies that suggested by the President's Fiscal Commission (fewer brackets, fewer deductions and credits, lower marginal rates) by proposing an end of the corporate income tax, making dividends and capital gains taxable as normal income, increasing the highest marginal tax rate (that would still be lower than today's top rate), and reinstating a federal inheritance tax.

The Challenge

Both sides have managed big electoral victories in the last few years, mostly by exploiting the weaknesses of the other. "I am not as bad as them" may work quite well politically for some time to come, and may even be both sides best bet for the 2012 election. And there is great uncertainty in taking the bold step of moving beyond vague generalities about a balanced budget and getting down the reality of the hard choices required on taxes and spending. If Progressives lead the charge to not only talk about a balanced budget, but to propose a vision of how to get there, we may be rewarded electorally. However, it is possible that we will not be.

It is true that Progressives have more to lose in the short term, notably the Senate and the Presidency. However, the biggest losers if there is no substantial movement between now and the next election toward developing a long-term sustainable budget are my children and grandchildren who have yet to be born (and yours). We Progressives should take a chance, for them, because there are worse things than losing elections.

Chapter 2
Why the Deficit Is a Problem

Since I was born in 1967, there have only been 4 years in which the US government took in as much money in taxes as it spent: 1969, 1998, 1999, and 2000. In the other 40 years, the federal government of the United States had an annual budget deficit. The government was able to spend more than it took in because it could easily borrow the money necessary to make up the shortfall by issuing government bonds, which simply means that investors loan money to the government, and in return, the government agrees to pay investors interest and principal over a specified period of time. The federal government pays the lowest possible interest rate because it has never failed to pay creditors the interest they were due. Even with the debt ceiling debate, the interest rate the US government is currently paying on our debt is very low.

Each annual budget deficit adds to the cumulative debt of the US government. Our revolutionary founding fathers borrowed money from France and the Netherlands to finance war against England. The US government first officially borrowed money in 1790 to make these war debts the responsibility of the US government, and the federal government has been in debt ever since. We don't have to repay all of our debts in a set period of time because we can easily refinance our debt, but we do have to pay interest on time in order to keep our good credit rating. The cumulative debt of the US is around $15 trillion or nearly $50,000 per capita in January 2012.

Even though having a federal budget deficit has become the norm in modern society, the size and the reason for future deficits make taking public policy steps to address the budget deficit a public policy priority.

There are three reasons that projected deficits present a problem:

First, deficits going forward will be large primarily due to the payment of predictable governmental expenses such as Medicare and Medicaid, Social Security and Defense with our current tax structure. Deficit financing is an important tool to maintain for emergencies, but it is inappropriate to use sustained, large-scale deficit financing for predictable expenses.

Second, a predictably large deficit crowds out the ability of the federal government to undertake important tasks, such as short term efforts to improve the economy, or investing in Progressive priorities such as infrastructure, education, energy, and the environment. Even if the sums of money needed for such projects is relatively small, so long as the political discussion of deficits is apocalyptic but yields no solutions, it will remain hard to successfully argue for Progressive priorities that require governmental funding.

Third, the key safety net programs of Medicare, Medicaid, and Social Security are at the heart of the unsustainability of the current benefit and spending structure of the federal budget. This means these programs will be changed, it is only a matter of when and how. Progressives should drive the changes in order to have maximum influence on the outcome.

How Big Is Too Big?

The best way to represent the amount of money owed (debt) by the federal government is to express it as a percentage of 1 year's total economic output of the nation—the Gross Domestic Product (GDP). Exactly what constitutes "too large" is unclear, but as the cumulative debt rises above 100% of GDP, most think this level is not sustainable over the long term. The way that a large cumulative debt harms the economy is the increase in interest costs that must be paid, diverting money from more productive uses. Eventually this will harm the economy. The cumulative debt is approaching 100% of GDP, but interest rates are very low mitigating the short-term impact on our finances. In a decade or so with no action, and a normally functioning economy, the cumulative debt will be similar in size to what it was just after World War II (around 125% of GDP). Interest payments will divert money from more productive uses, and our economy will be vulnerable to any increase in interest rates.

Generally, annual budget deficits rise during times of war (e.g., World War II or the wars in Iraq and Afghanistan), or a very poor economy (e.g., the Great Depression or the most recent recession) and fall or remain stable during times of peace and more rapid growth of the economy. The peak level of cumulative indebtedness of our nation was just after World War II when we owed around 125% of GDP. That means we owed 25% more than the entire value of our economy in 1950. Thus, the United States had a more serious debt situation in 1950 than it does today.

However, the amount owed (represented as the percent of GDP) declined steadily in the 30 years following World War II because the rate of economic growth was larger than the rate of borrowing undertaken by the federal government during this period of time. In other words, the overall economy grew faster than did the amount we were deficit financing in each year. Since taxes received are related to the size of the economy, the cumulative debt of the nation can actually fall in percent of GDP terms even as we continue to have annual budget deficits that are relatively small, at least compared to the growth rate of the economy. This is what happened during the 1950s–1970s.

The cumulative debt as a percentage of GDP grew during the 1980s and declined during the 1990s as we actually had three of the four balanced budgets in the last 40 years in 1998–2000. The debt began to grow more rapidly in the 2000s, and rose very quickly in the past 3 years due to the severity of the economic crisis which meant lower than expected tax receipts and higher than typical government spending.

The projected budget deficits over the next several decades are unsustainable and warrant public policy attention because they will be very large due to the predictable costs of health care and retirement for the aging baby boomers given our default tax structure. Historically deficits rose only in times of war or economic crisis. Without substantial policy changes, they will rise rapidly due to cost increases of predictable spending, pushing our cumulative debt toward dangerous levels going forward as a matter of course, even with good economic growth in the economy. Our current federal budget is unsustainable over the long run.

The Mere Existence of a Deficit Is Not Evidence of a Problem

Hyperbole on the deficit is not the same as good policy. If so, we would have no problem, because we have far more hysterical talk than practical policy discussion that could actually address the problem. We need to react, but it is important not to overreact, and it is crucial to undertake the correct policy changes that will address our deficit over the long run, while not harming our economy in the short run.

It is important to realize that there will be times when running even a large deficit is necessary and good policy. The mere existence of a deficit is not proof of a problem, and policy remedies such as a balanced budget amendment that would rid us of this policy tool amount to getting out of the ditch on one side of the road, and going into the one on the other side. However, the best way to argue against bad ideas such as a balanced budget amendment is to take action and develop a long-range plan to move toward a balanced and sustainable budget.

The Kitchen Table

The metaphor that is often used to describe the budget deficit is that of a family budget discussion around the proverbial kitchen table. In one sense this is a fair analogy, but in another it is false.

Most families are in debt, and they must decide if continued borrowing (running a family deficit) is worth it. In the same way, the federal government must decide if continued deficit financing on our current path given our current circumstances is worth it. For example, I live in a house with my family that was purchased with a mortgage. I pay interest and principal to the bank each month and over a period of 30 years will pay far more for the right to live in my house than I would have if I paid cash the day I moved in. However, I didn't have that much cash, so the only choices were to either not live in my house, or to borrow the money to enable me to do so. Was this a good decision? Are the financing costs worth it?

This is of course a value judgment. Most people will likely think that my decision to buy a house via borrowing money is a better decision than splurging on a fancy vacation that was debt financed. However, my housing decision seems less clear that it did even 3 years ago given what has happened to housing prices. Even so, while the judgment is subjective, most persons would think of the purchase of a house as an investment, while the choice to finance a vacation via debt would be seen as a luxury that would not be "worth it." There are of course more difficult decisions. Is it worth it to borrow money for a college degree? Does the cost of such a degree from Duke University, where I teach, warrant a price tag that is three times larger than that of the University of North Carolina, where I earned my college degree? The same sorts of questions can and should be asked about the source of government deficits.

In another sense, the family kitchen table is a poor analogy for the US government's debt situation, and the way the metaphor tends to be used politically to argue against deficit spending is false. The image is of a family tightening its budget belt in hard times, which of course many families are doing today. However, if they have a mortgage, they most certainly do not have a "balanced budget" even after such a family discussion. Further, if the US government acted in austerity to each economic downturn, then this would make such downturns even worse. This points out the reality that the US government is different from individual households, and can borrow money in perpetuity and therefore finance consumption that would otherwise be impossible, so long as we don't borrow *too much* and the reasons for deficit financing are good ones.

Paying for predictable governmental responsibilities is not a good reason for ongoing and large deficit financing.

Fast Forward to 2020

Generalities can only get you so far in a discussion of the deficit, or any other type of consequential public policy. Let's look at the 2010 federal budget and what it is likely to look like in 2020 given some politically plausible scenarios (extend the current tax code until then) to demonstrate why the budget deficit presents a unique problem in the US history, that nevertheless can and should be addressed while advancing progressive priorities.

The federal budget deficit in 2010 was $1.3 trillion, and will be of similar size in 2011. This simply means that the federal government spent $1.3 trillion more in 2010 than we collected in taxes. The deficit is simply the difference between the "ins and the outs." The "ins" are taxes, and the "outs" are government spending and aspects of the tax code that benefit one group of taxpayers over another via the so-called tax expenditures. Direct spending is easier to understand, so let's start there.

In Fiscal Year 2010, around two-thirds of the federal budget was spent on just five line items

Military, $663 billion (20%)
Social Security, $695 billion (20%)
Medicare, $453 billion (14%)
Medicaid, $290 billion (7%)
Interest on the debt, $164 billion (6%)

The top four items are fairly self-explanatory. Interest payments on the cumulative national debt are also a large item, and the more money that is owed, the higher will interest payments be. Interest payments on the national debt are not discretionary, and must be paid to keep the US government from going into default (not paying its creditors), which would certainly set off a worldwide economic crisis. It would also certainly lead to an increase in the interest rate that we had to offer for new borrowing (government bonds), further worsening the problem. As interest payments increase, that diverts money from other potential uses.

The other items are both large and important, and are also entirely predictable. Article I, Section 8 of the Constitution explicitly names "Common Defence" of the nation as a responsibility of the federal government of the United States. The amount that we spend on the military is a choice, but the budget category is ongoing and predictable, and we have long spent the most of any nation on defense (by far).

The next three items comprise the basis of our social safety net. Social Security, which provides retirement benefits and other protections such as disability payments to those who cannot work before retirement age and to children who are orphaned, has been in place since 1935. Around one in ten elderly persons have no retirement income other than Social Security, and another one in four receive 90% of their income from Social Security. Medicare and Medicaid, which pay for health care services of the elderly and the poor, respectively, were created in 1965. The cost of these important programs is totally predictable under current policy, and our society expects such programs.

The 111th Congress extended the current income tax rates for 2 years. If those same tax rates are kept through 2020, and there are no major changes to the spending side of the equation, the deficit in that year will be over $1 trillion even if a normally functioning and growing economy is in place. The percentage of the federal budget that is consumed by the Medicare program alone in 2020 will be 20% instead of 14% in 2010. Our projected interest payments on the debt in 2020 will equal nearly $1 trillion for that year alone, around the same amount we will pay for Medicare. Even more instructive is the fact that the total spent on the five line items above will exceed the tax receipts of the federal government in that year.

If we extend the current tax rates indefinitely and make no other consequential policy changes, every dollar spent in the 2020 budget that is not spent on the military, Social Security, Medicare and Medicaid, and interest payments on the debt will be borrowed. To put it another way, we would still have a budget deficit even if we eradicated *all* federal spending other than the five line items if the current tax code remains in place. No NIH. No Homeland Security. No FBI. Nothing other than those five budget items and we would still have a deficit.

We are on auto pilot for very large deficits that will push our cumulative debt toward levels that will harm our economy. And that is without an economic crisis or another war, but simply due to paying for programs that are completely predictable and costly.

Deficits Crowd Out Progressive Priorities

The federal Department of Education is relatively small, with an annual budget of $46 billion in 2010, out of a total federal budget of $3.5 trillion. A high profile program called "Race to the Top" is the type of program that could be considered an investment, in that it is a new program that is designed to boost academic achievement which is hoped to lead to improved economic development down the road. Similarly, President Obama is proposing expanded federal spending on high speed rail infrastructure, with a request of around $60 billion over 8 years made in the 2011 State of the Union speech. This too is best thought of as an investment since the goal is new spending to boost infrastructure, which will hopefully increase economic development.

The federal government can undertake spending of this type, which represents a large amount of money in absolute terms, that is, nevertheless, a small proportion of the federal budget. Conceptually, that is no different from you or me borrowing money to buy a car or a house. Questions about the wisdom of such programs or whether the federal government should undertake these types of efforts is a legitimate source of debate and discussion. Are they worth it? Part of the answer is that the government can easily borrow money for such initiatives at the lowest possible interest rate because the credit markets assume it to be a nearly risk-free source of interest for those seeking safe savings options. However, very large and predictable deficits that will push our debt toward dangerous levels crowd out the ability to undertake such governmental projects.

Similarly, the current focus on deficit reduction but without agreeing to a long-range plan has also crowded out discussion of further government spending to stimulate jobs and the weak economy. Whether such intervention came in the form aid to states to support state government jobs that are being cut, further intervention into the mortgage crisis, or other efforts, such initiatives do not seem to be viewed as realistic because of the degree to which the rhetoric of deficit reduction has heightened awareness of the issue, while our political system has so far proven unable to develop a long-range plan.

Not If, but When?

We do not need to immediately balance our budget, and doing so with large cuts to governmental services and discretionary spending would actually be bad for our fragile economy. What we do need is a plan, and a path toward a sustainable and balanced budget. This will give investors more confidence that the United States will be able to pay its bills, keeping interest rates as low as possible as we move toward a sustainable federal budget. Absent such a plan, we will eventually have a debt crisis that would likely begin with investors being unwilling to loan us more money out of fears that we would be unable to pay it back. We would have to offer higher interest rates to tempt investors, touching off a vicious cycle that would likely lead to austere budget cuts far more draconian than what would come about as part of a long-range deficit reduction plan.

It is not clear when such a debt crisis will emerge or exactly what will trigger it. We are not in one now, so there is time to make a long-range plan in a reasoned fashion. If we do not develop a long-range plan for a balanced budget, we will likely find out sometime in the next decade what such a crisis looks like.

This book makes some practical policy arguments that would move us toward a sustainable federal budget, which means stabilizing the deficit in the short term, and moving over the medium and long term to developing balanced federal budgets. The book focuses on health care, because our deficit problem is most fundamentally a health care cost problem. But, it touches on the other big parts of the equation: Social Security, defense, and the tax code side of the equation that determines how much revenue comes into the federal treasury.

There are some who say that the US government should always have a small federal deficit (say 0.5% of GDP) because this allows for the financing of consumption that improves quality of life for our people to levels that would otherwise be unachievable. In economic terms this is true, and I probably agree. However, my response to that argument is let's get our deficit to this low level on a predictable basis and then have that debate.

To get anywhere near a balanced budget at some point in the future will require profound health care reform beyond that as passed in the Affordable Care Act. The next five chapters lay out the nature of the health care problem and provide a practical way forward, because slowing the rate of health care cost inflation is a necessary, but not a sufficient condition to ever having a balanced budget. Put another way, if you hear a politician say that balancing the budget is their top priority you should ask them one question. "What is your health reform plan?"

Chapter 3
Health Reform: The Problems

When teaching my introductory health policy class at Duke University, I begin the first day by describing two "laws" that I believe govern all health care systems:

Everyone dies
Before that, the healthy subsidize the sick

The first point is a fact. The second implies a choice (or many choices). The essence of health policy is working out how the healthy will subsidize the sick. We return throughout the semester to these laws as we work through many wonky details such as whether insurance companies are allowed to deny insurance coverage based on preexisting conditions, whether older persons are charged higher premiums than are younger ones in employer-based insurance, and whether there are lifetime maximum benefits in Medicare or private insurance. Each of these policy choices is simply a different way of deciding how the healthy will (and will not) subsidize the sick.

When talking with community groups about health policy and suggesting these two organizing themes, it is interesting how much nervous laughter there is when noting the obvious fact that everyone dies. This holds true even for groups of physicians and health care providers; quick looks left and right when noting the obvious. It is not surprising for my 19-year-old students to laugh off death, but what about retirement age groups and physicians? The problem with not really getting the first point is that it likely influences our views about the second one in ways that we don't fully understand. Some type of subsidy of the sick by the well is inevitable, but what form shall the subsidy take?

Just because such subsidy is inevitable doesn't mean it is not controversial. The political and legal fight surrounding whether an individual mandate imposed by the federal government to force the purchase of health insurance is constitutional is really a question about the legitimacy of this approach to the healthy subsidizing the sick. Similarly, asking whether it is reasonable to use cuts in planned Medicare spending to finance insurance expansions is also a question about whether this means of the healthy subsidizing the sick is legitimate, or a good idea. Even if we decided not to expand health insurance coverage and required the uninsured to rely upon charity if they cannot pay for care on an out of pocket basis, this is still a statement of how (voluntary action) the healthy will subsidize the sick.

The subsidy of the sick by the healthy did not start with the Affordable Care Act (ACA). A few examples are likely so ingrained in our consciousness that we pay them little attention.

The US Medicare program lumps all persons age 65 and older into one insurance risk pool that includes around 45 million persons. A few use very large amounts of care while others use only a small amount, and a very few use none in a given year. Around 60% of the program's annual expenditures are spent on 10% of beneficiaries; at the other end of the spectrum, half of those covered by Medicare use just 3% of its annual total spending. The annual premium paid by these two groups for the doctor insurance portion of Medicare (Part B) is identical for most beneficiaries, even though their use of care is very different. In this way, the healthy subsidize the sick within the Medicare program in a given year.

Let's assume two Medicare beneficiaries had the same earnings history over their working years, and therefore paid the same amount in Medicare payroll taxes prior to becoming eligible for the program. However, one has a series of strokes and numerous hospitalizations, while the other is vigorous and healthy and dies in his sleep at the same age as the other dies in a hospital. Two people who paid the same amount in Medicare payroll taxes over the course of their working life, lived to the same age, but who had very different uses of health care. Again, the healthy subsidize the sick.

The same principle is found in private health insurance. Duke University provides health insurance to me as a benefit of my employment, and it covers me, my wife, and three children. Duke pays a premium of around $580 per month for this policy; I pay a monthly premium of $322. The policy that Duke has arranged stipulates that all Duke employees choosing family coverage are charged the same premium, regardless of the age, health, or number of persons covered by their particular policy. If a professor has cancer, he or she does not pay a higher premium than a professor who does not. If one family has one child and another has five, they pay the same family premium.

This is called community rating, which means that the premium charged is based on an overall average instead of setting premiums based on an individual's likelihood of needing care in a given year. The structure of Duke's insurance offerings is the choice of Duke. They could choose to charge employees different premiums based on their health, but instead they choose community rating. Why? Because it is simple and reduces administrative costs that would rise if each person was charged a risk-based premium. Such an approach works because the size of the risk pool is large, which simply means there are numerous healthy persons to subsidize those who are sick within the risk pool. The larger the risk pool, the less the potential benefit for underwriting to Duke (or the insurer). And Duke has a large risk pool (around 33,000 employees).

Around 51 million persons were uninsured in 2011. Some of them are young and well, and it is probably not a big deal to be uninsured so long as they are not in a car

Health Reform: The Problems

accident or don't have another unexpected health event, like finding a lump in their breast. However, some of the uninsured are sick or do get injured in an accident and often face bankruptcy trying to pay their medical bills. Our nation has a strong cultural norm that could be called the rescue principle—you help those in need—even if they cannot pay. This norm was reaffirmed in law in 1986 through the Emergency Medical Treatment and Active Labor Act (EMTALA). EMTALA stipulates that care must be provided to those needing it in an emergency room, even if they cannot pay. Hospitals typically seek to collect the cost of this care from patients who are uninsured, and many individuals go bankrupt trying to pay their bills, ruining their credit. However, much of the total is unrecovered because very few people have a hope of paying the cost of medical care in the absence of health insurance, because the care is so expensive. This unrecovered cost is paid for by society in a variety of ways:

By those with private health insurance through higher premiums, which are increased because private insurance pays more than it otherwise would for care to offset the uncompensated care that is incurred by hospitals and physicians. This is called cost shifting.

By taxpayers who foot the bill for local and state government contributions to hospitals that provide a good deal of the care to the uninsured via emergency rooms.

Via higher cost of the Medicare and Medicaid programs through the payment of disproportionate share (DSH) payments that are made to hospitals by these government insurance programs to hospitals that provide a large amount of health care to the uninsured, and extra payments to teaching hospitals whose resident physicians often staff emergency rooms.

In all of these ways and many others, the healthy (and the insured) subsidize the sick (and the uninsured).

The healthy subsidize the sick in other nations as well. The English National Health Service (NHS) places all of its residents into one insurance pool like Duke University places all employees in one pool. The NHS is an example of community rating on a national level, all 34 million people in one pool. The NHS then provides access to the health care system as a matter of right, with little cost share at the time care is used, with the cost of the system financed by both income and consumption taxes. Persons who pay little in taxes receive access to care just as do those with who pay more in taxes to finance the NHS. Likewise, persons who are sick receive more care than do those who are well, no matter how much each paid in taxes to finance the NHS the previous year. The healthy subsidize the sick.

All of the high income democracies of the world other than the United States. have developed a means of providing health insurance coverage to all their citizens. The policy details of how each nation sets up health insurance, financing and the delivery of care differs, but at the most basic level, all of these schemes have the practical effect of the healthy subsidizing the sick. They do not differ in that some do this and others do not, they differ in *how they do it*. And as described above, not developing a system of universal insurance coverage in the United States, we have simply made other provisions for how the healthy will subsidize the sick, though many of the relationships may not be obvious, result in poor access to care and outcomes, and represent an inefficient means of cross subsidization.

The healthy subsidizing the sick is not a new idea, nor a creation of modern society; human interactions have long had the effect of offering care to those who needed help, and who were helpless. In a nomadic hunter/gatherer society in which most persons spent most of their energy obtaining food for the next day, if you were sick and couldn't hunt and gather, you died unless someone brought you food. Whatever motivation you ascribe to why the healthy brought food to the sick in such a society, this behavior has been observed in many forms across many years and societies. Modern health policy financing is just another example, a modern extension of this basic principle of being human.

The healthy subsidizing the sick is not unique to health care, and in one sense it is just the practical definition of insurance. Insurance is the trading of a predictable payment (premium) for protection against an unknown and potentially catastrophic harm or loss. The insurer who accepts the premium has become at risk for paying for the catastrophic loss should it occur (such as your car if you crash). For insurance markets to work, the aggregate receipt of premiums must cover the aggregate amount paid out by insurance companies, at least over long periods of time. If they do not, then the insurance company would go bankrupt. Similarly, if a public insurer pays out more than it takes in, either the ins must rise or the outs must drop, or deficit financing must be undertaken.

Homeowners insurance works because premiums are set at a level that covers losses due to fire, hail, flood, etc. If the house of everyone covered by State Farm Insurance Company burned down in a given year, then State Farm would be in serious trouble and might go bankrupt, because the premiums paid are very small in relation to the cost of a total loss. Someone's house (in fact most people's given the premium paid per insured dollar) has to not burn down in a given year for that insurance market to work. The basic principle is the same for car insurance, and every other type of insurance that you can imagine. There have to be those who pay premiums and who do not make claims for the insurance market to remain solvent and continue to operate. In this way, the "healthy" subsidize the "sick" in any type of insurance market. However, you only know after the fact, or period of insurance coverage, which group is which.

In all of the examples provided, those who are well may seem to get a bad deal, but you never know when you will shift from one group to the other.

However, there is one major difference between health care and other types of insurance, like homeowners insurance. Most people never have the experience of having their home burn. However, almost no one lives their entire life without using health care. Eventually, even the well use substantial amounts of health care services, with the rate of use rapidly increasing as people age and became sick, and inevitably approach death.

And everyone dies.

The Problems

There are three basic problems with the US health care system. First, it costs too much and is unsustainable given our current system of taxation and other spending priorities. Second, we have millions of persons without health insurance at a point in time, and many more who are exposed to being uninsured for periods of time because of the link between employment and health insurance in our nation. This leads to a variety of negative consequences, both for individuals as well as the overall health care system. Third, there are problems with the quality and appropriateness of the care provided. This has both human and financial costs. We need a reform approach that addresses each of these problems, because they are related.

Problem Number 1: Cost

The long term budget deficit problem facing our nation is primarily a health care cost problem. Put simply, getting a handle on health care costs is a necessary, but not a sufficient, condition for our nation to have any hope of developing a long-term balanced budget. If we manage to slow the health care cost growth rate to manageable levels, then we have a chance to develop a sustainable federal budget if we make wise decisions in developing a new tax code and setting parameters on other spending. If we deal with health care costs, we *can* address our nation's impending fiscal crisis. However, if we don't address health care costs and slow its rate of growth, it doesn't matter what else we do, we will not achieve a balanced budget.

We have the following four general approaches for dealing with the cost of our health care system and its impact on the federal budget:

Addressing health care costs by slowing their rate of inflation as compared to overall inflation

Increasing taxes to pay for the federal government's share of health care

Substantially decreasing other federal spending so that we can spend more of our federal budget on health care

Paying for the increasing federal share of health care costs by using deficit financing

These choices are all either bad or hard, or both, depending upon your perspective. I believe that we must address health care costs (option 1 above), not by seeking to spend less on health care, but by spending less in the future than our current path suggests we will spend. In other words, we need to slow the rate of growth in health care costs. To do so means that less care will be provided and/or providers will be paid less for the care provided than would otherwise occur in the default case. Whether you favor expert-based rationing of care or the use of markets to reduce costs, the last step of these polar-opposite approaches is the same if they are to work: less care will be delivered, and/or less will be paid to providers for the same care, as compared to continuing on the default track.

I do believe taxes must rise overall if we are to achieve a balanced budget, however, raising them enough to pay for the default level of health care costs implied by our system is unrealistic, and would entrench some poor quality, inappropriate, or ineffective care. If we could get to the point where health care costs went up one percentage point faster than GDP growth in the long run it would be the greatest public policy achievement in the history of the United States. This is a simple objective, but will be very hard to achieve.

How Did We Get Here?

In 2010, the United States spent around $2.5 trillion on health care, or an average of $8,500 per person. This doesn't mean each person received $8,500 worth of health care, that is simply the per capita expenditure (total divided by population). This represented 17.5% of our nation's GDP, which means that one in six dollars in our economy was spent on health care last year. In 1980 we spent $1,072 per capita or 8.8% of GDP on health care. So both the amount spent on health care is rising as is the share of our economy that is devoted to health care.

In 1994, after the demise of the Clinton health reform plan, I had informal discussions with health policy graduate students and professors in my graduate school program in which we agreed that there was no way that health spending could go above 12–13% of GDP; we thought it represented some sort of natural cap (I don't remember why we thought this, but graduate students are sometimes right but never in doubt). Obviously this was wrong, and it appears there may be no limit to what our nation can spend on health care. The United States has long spent the most on health care of any nation in the world, and our health expenditures alone are larger than the entire economy of most nations. We spend more per capita on health care than China's entire GDP per capita. In and of itself, spending a lot on health care proves nothing. Maybe we simply prefer health spending to other types of spending and are willing to invest more of our money in it as compared to other things.

This is a legitimate perspective, and in a democratic society we could decide that we would invest more of the federal budget in health care, and less in other things, or raise taxes to pay for health care. However, we have not done the second or third part—spend less on other things, or raise taxes to pay for health care. And as the baby boomers begin to move into eligibility for Medicare, our autopilot level of spending will greatly increase the federal share of the health care costs of our nation. This is going to lead to predictably large budget deficits to pay for the cost of Medicare and Medicaid.

Considering how much we spend per capita as compared to other nations provides a more legitimate comparison through which to evaluate the performance of our health care system. The amount of money spent per capita is not uniformly spent across individuals in the United States, but this is true of other nations as well. In 1980, we spent $1.50 per capita each time our cultural and economic partners spent $1; today this has risen to around $2 while these nations spend $1, so our real expenditure on health care services per capita has risen much faster than in other nations. On the whole, the outcomes our nation achieves are basically average when compared to the other high income nations of the world; better in some areas, worse in others. Yet, we spend twice as much. This raises serious questions about whether we are getting our money's worth for what we spend on health care, and points out what I call the good bad news: since we spend a great deal on health care that appears to be non productive, we should be able to reduce our rate of health care cost inflation without harming patients. In fact, it should be possible, but not easy, to improve the quality and appropriateness of care while reducing costs.

Who Pays for Health Care?

Just under one in two dollars spent on health care is paid for directly by government, or around $1 trillion in 2010. A large portion of this is paid for by Medicare, which had a 2010 budget of around $500 billion, followed by the federal portion of Medicaid, which was around $300 billion. States are responsible for funding a portion of their Medicaid program, and cumulatively spent around $200 billion on Medicaid in 2010. The federal government also directly pays for the Veterans Administration health system and some other smaller direct care provision programs such as the Indian Health Service. These figures represent the default before the passage of the ACA, and the income-based premium subsidies to help persons purchase private health insurance beginning in 2014 will add another source of direct federal spending on health care.

In fact, our public expenditures alone on health care services are greater than the total health spending (public and private) of many nations. And we have even higher levels of per capita private health care expenditures paid by private health insurance and out of pocket payment for care.

I use the phrase direct federal spending because private insurance is heavily subsidized by the federal government via the preferential tax treatment of employer-based health insurance, which will be more fully discussed later. This is a fundamental attribute of the US health care system. The dollar value of this tax benefit to people like me with employer-based private health insurance was around $250 billion in 2010. To restate, if there were no preferential tax treatment of employer-paid insurance premiums (which benefits those with good employer based policies), then the federal deficit would have been $250 billion lower in 2010 than it was. Again, this is the default system that was in place prior to the passage of the ACA, and is a cornerstone of the employer-based insurance system.

Another way of parsing health care spending is by type of care. The largest line items are hospital, physician, and pharmaceuticals. Interestingly, this rank order holds in all high income nations, so the primary differences across nations in spending are the level, not the relative weighting of costs at the macrolevel. Further, out of pocket expenditures—meaning patients paying for care not covered at all or fully by insurance—are a part of just about all health care systems in high income nations, and tend to aggregate around 10% of total health system spending.

The growth in Medicare (and to a lesser extent, Medicaid) is the main source of the projected federal budget deficit problem over the next few decades. However, the United States has a general health care cost problem that is shared by both Medicare and private insurance. Both have risen much faster than general inflation in the past. There are periods of time when the rate of inflation in private insurance has been slightly higher, and others when it is the opposite, but they are fairly closely linked over time. The US health care system has a cost problem, not one payer or another.

This makes sense because we don't have a separate health care delivery system for private insurance and Medicare. Physicians and hospitals tend to treat both privately insured patients as well as Medicare beneficiaries, though there are differences across specialty. A *pediatrician* is not likely to treat many Medicare beneficiaries (though some children are permanently disabled and eligible for Medicare), and a *urologist* is likely to see many Medicare beneficiaries. There are issues that Medicaid beneficiaries face in not being able to find private physicians to be their doctor due to the relatively low payment rates. However, virtually no hospital would refuse Medicaid, and would greatly prefer it to attempting to collect on a bill that was owed by a person who was uninsured.

The reason that health care cost inflation is a problem for the federal budget is that in Medicare we join our general cost inflation problem with the demographic change known as the baby boomers. As the baby boomers move into Medicare eligibility beginning now, they obtain access to health insurance that is primarily financed by taxes. Thus, the share of the health care cost bill to be paid by the federal government will grow rapidly in the next decade leading to large deficits with no change due to the baby boomers moving into Medicare eligibility and the fact that health care is so expensive in the United States.

It is important to keep in mind the difference between cost shifting and cost reduction. If our singular aim is the federal budget deficit, then a program such as the one proposed by Representative Ryan in April 2011 to provide vouchers for private insurance that are insufficient to purchase benefits similar to those provided by Medicare, and therefore shift costs to the elderly could suffice (he has since moderated this proposal via the so-called Wyden–Ryan plan, discussed later). In my mind, while the federal budget deficit drives our need to reform the health care system, the goal is a sustainable health care system, which means a level of expenditures that is broadly understood to be appropriate, and for which we are willing to pay. To achieve this will require spending less than what will be provided by default, meaning the delivery of less care and/or the payment of less to providers for the same care. This will be very hard to do.

Big Problem Number 2: Lack of Coverage

A second problem with the US health care system is the large number of uninsured persons. This is not a short-term problem, but one that is perpetual and inevitable given our current system. During the health reform debate, some persons were more focused on this issue than the problem of costs. For many, the lack of a straightforward means of insuring every person in a nation that is as rich as ours is a profound moral failure. For others, addressing the problem of the uninsured by developing a mechanism for guaranteed coverage is a matter of efficiency; since we have a system in which the uninsured often get care, although often late, it often comes in the most expensive setting (emergency room) and results in some costs being shifted to private insurance in ways that are difficult to appropriately account for. In either event, the presence of the uninsured is relevant to the cost discussion, and certainly to attempts to slow the rate of cost inflation.

Around three in six Americans (155–160 million persons) are covered by private health insurance, mostly provided by an employer as a benefit of employment. This includes dependent children.

Two in six are covered by government health insurance, namely 45 million persons the Medicare program that covers all persons who are age 65 and above as well as persons with end stage renal (kidney) disease and those who are permanently disabled. Approximately 60–65 million persons are covered by Medicaid, which is the joint federal/state insurance program that covers persons with low income. The number of persons who are eligible for Medicaid tends to rise during economic downturns as people lose their job and health insurance. The eligibility rules and benefit design differ by state, but most persons covered by Medicaid are pregnant women and children, in large part due to expansion of eligibility rules for pregnant women over the past 15–20 years as a means of addressing the problem of inadequate prenatal care and subsequent poor birth outcomes.

Most political and even policy discussion assumes that Medicaid is a homogenous group of patients, "the poor." Nothing could be further from the truth. In fact, I think of Medicaid as three distinct programs, meaning groups of beneficiaries whose needs and realities are very different.

Program 1: covers mainly pregnant women and children for acute services. There are around *45–50 million* such persons. The ACA would greatly expand this portion of the program. This is the group that experienced barriers to access in the recent study, and this is where most of the debate is centered. Such beneficiaries are numerous, but are relatively inexpensive on a per capita basis.

Program 2: covers long-term care, most notably nursing home care for Medicare beneficiaries who are also poor and therefore covered by Medicaid. Such persons are known as Dual Eligibles because they are covered by both Medicare and Medicaid. There are *nine million* duals, around two-thirds of them are eligible for Medicare because of age, the remainder due to permanent disability. This relatively small number of persons are extremely costly to both Medicare and Medicaid.

Program 3: covers long term care and acute specialized services for persons younger than 65 who are disabled, but not eligible for Medicare; There are *five million* such persons, who are not as homogenous due to their variety of needs.

Most of the discussion of Medicaid is related to program 1 above or acute care Medicaid. This is especially true given the use of Medicaid expansions to provide coverage increases in the ACA. However, it is important to remember that the Medicaid program insures a diverse group of persons, including the many children who are relatively healthy as well as some of the most vulnerable members of our society. Group 1 is much less expensive than groups 2 and 3 on a per capita basis. I will provide more detail about these three groups of Medicaid beneficiaries and my proposal for reforming Medicaid later.

Of course, that leaves one in six Americans who are uninsured at a given time. The existence of such a large proportion of the population that does not have health insurance is one of the most notable descriptors of our health care system. Who are they?

First, they are younger than age 65, since the Medicare program provides universal coverage at that age and older.

Second, they are people who either do not have access to job-based health insurance, or who have declined an offer to purchase job-based health insurance, typically because the employee share of the premiums is viewed as too high. Most persons who are uninsured at a given point in time have a job or are the child of someone who is employed. Over time, the link between employment and insurance is breaking down. From 2009 to 2010, the number of persons with employer-based coverage actually declined, for the first time since the Census Bureau tracked the uninsured. This was due in large part to the very severe economic downturn, but there is a trend over time for employers to move toward contract employees and part time workers, at least in part to avoid the benefit costs associated with private health insurance. Only a minority of persons are uninsured for longer than 6 months, while others move in and out of coverage, often due to job changes, though this is likely changing during the current economic downturn due to long-term unemployment.

Third, they are persons who are not poor enough to qualify for Medicaid. Children have the lowest rate of being uninsured than any age group other than the elderly. Many are insured via a job of their parent, but the expansion of Medicaid through what are known as State Child Health Insurance Program (SCHIP) initiatives have greatly reduced the rate of being uninsured among children. Women who are pregnant are also less likely to be uninsured because of Medicaid coverage expansions in the 1990s that expanded coverage eligibility for pregnant women out of concerns around the health effects of children born without receiving prenatal care. Thus, the story of pregnant women and children demonstrates that policy choice can reduce the uninsured, even within our existing system.

There were around 51 million persons with no health insurance at a given time during 2010. Most of these persons were not uninsured for the entire year (but around one in four were) but instead moved in and out of insurance often due to a change in job. While persons who are age 65 and over and those with low income are covered by Medicare and Medicaid, most persons receive health insurance as a benefit of employment. That means that having a job that provides health insurance is how most Americans are covered, including dependent children. My job as a Professor at Duke University provides health insurance coverage for five people: my wife and me and our three children. If I lost my job, then we would eventually lose our health insurance.

Persons who are uninsured tend to get care, but often receive it late, and in settings that are very expensive, such as emergency rooms. There are both legal and cultural mores that dictate that persons receive some care even if they cannot pay. The end result is a subset of the population who suffer from delayed or foregone care, poorer quality care, worse outcomes and many persons who are financially devastated attempting to pay for health care bills that are run up due to not having health insurance. In fact, persons who are uninsured are typically charged the highest price for care, far more than an insurance company that can negotiate a volume discount. Health care bills are the leading source of bankruptcy in the United States and figured heavily as a triggering event for the home loan foreclosure crisis.

Some view the cyclical nature of being uninsured as proving that the problem is overblown. The argument goes that most are not uninsured for years (which is true), but are instead uninsured for periods of time or spells, often around life changing events, such as graduating from college, aging out of your parents insurance policy, or changing jobs. But, others lose insurance because they become ill and can no longer work, ending their source of financing needed care.

Another way to view the cyclical nature of insurance is that this means that far more persons and a larger proportion of the population are exposed to a period of being uninsured. While 51 million were said to be uncovered at a point in time in 2010, around 80 million were uninsured for some period during the year. Because of the cyclical nature of being uninsured in the United States, more than one in four persons may be exposed to a spell of uninsurance in a given year.

A final problem with being uninsured comes about from the fact (legal and cultural) that persons tend to get some care even if uninsured. This means that the cost of uncompensated care (especially for hospitals) is shifted to other payers, such as private insurance companies. This in turn raises health insurance premiums for employers and employees, which leads to lower wages than an employee would otherwise have received. Precisely estimating the impact of such a cost shift is difficult, and there is some recent evidence showing that cost shifting is very complicated and may have a smaller direct impact than once thought.

There is a subtle aspect of the cost shifting that hinders our ability to comprehensively control health care cost inflation, above and beyond any direct cost increase imposed on others. If I run an insurance company and am attempting to negotiate the amount of money that I will pay to a hospital for a given service, say an appendectomy, the hospital negotiators will describe their inability to accept the price I say I want to pay and will almost certainly invoke the cost of uncompensated care in saying this. There is a real cost that is borne by the hospital for uncompensated care, which would legitimately affect their ability to accept a given price as payment for a service. However, I believe there is an extra "negotiation effect" whereby the hospital will use this (real) cost of uncompensated care, but will essentially claim the cost is higher than it actually is. Until all persons are insured (or the uninsured are turned away and not given care) it will be very hard to fully address health care cost inflation because the shifted costs are difficult to predict and identify in terms of their impact on the bottom line of a hospital or other provider.

Big Problem Number 3: Quality

There is a third fundamental problem with our health care system, and that is the quality of care provided to patients. All health systems have problems have multi-faceted quality problems, and ours is no different. There is a voluminous research literature on this topic that this book will not review. The main point for continued health reform is that even though we spend two times as much per capita as most nation's on health care, we have similar levels of quality, leading to the conclusion that the extra spending does not show itself in improved outcomes for our people. This means that it should be possible to reduce the rate of health care cost inflation while actually improving quality. In fact, without the requirement to reduce cost inflation, the inertia in the health care system might even make it harder to improve quality.

There are three basic types of quality problems. First, care that is provided erroneously, this is often described as the problem with medical errors such as operating on the wrong body part or giving the wrong medicine. A second type of quality problem is providing care that is inappropriate for the situation of the patient. The third type of quality problem is not providing care that is indicated by the patient's situation, such as not offering a screening test when one is indicated. Both the second and third problems signify a suboptimal mismatch between what a patient needed and what they got. Sometimes the patient gets too much, sometimes too little. Both are problems. Altogether, these quality problems demonstrate that we are not getting our money's worth for our large expenditures, and that we can do better.

Medical Errors

The 1999 Institute of Medicine report, *To Err Is Human*, greatly altered the debate on quality of care in the United States, and drew attention to quality shortcomings, especially problems associated with medical errors. This report estimated that around 98,000 persons died annually in the United States due to medical errors, a figure that would make errors among the ten leading causes of death in our nation. The report and follow-ups have of course been criticized. But, let's assume they over estimated the number of deaths related to medical errors by a factor of ten, and the true number is 9,800. Even then, that would mean that 27 people a day die of medical errors in the United States. It is hard to argue that is not alarming, and a problem. A variety of high profile efforts have been undertaken to address errors and some simple procedures such as checklists prior to surgery have shown some promise and ability to improve quality in certain surgical care. In November 2010, a study in the *New England Journal of Medicine* demonstrated that major hospital error rates remained essentially unchanged in a sample of North Carolina hospitals. Thus, the last 10 years have seen an explosion in the discussion of the quality problem in the US health care system, an increase in efforts to improve it, and limited evidence that it has gotten any better.

Inappropriate Provision of Care

Both of the other two types of quality problems amount to the improper provision of health care to patients given their needs and preferences. Sometimes patients received too little care, sometimes too much. For example, a NEJM paper by Elizabeth McGlynn and others several years back noted that adults only receive around half of the services that would be understood to be optimal quality during a primary care visit. This type of research is controversial because it applies guidelines for what patients should receive to actual care, and many rightly note that it would be impossible for a primary care physician to provide the "optimal" level of suggested screening and prevention in a 15 minutes office visit. However measured, one issue is patients not receiving care that would have helped them. Not receiving warranted care could sometimes increase costs long term, and other times might not.

Overprovision of care can also be an issue of quality. There is a strong assumption in our nation and culture that more is always better and some care is provided that may actually reduce quality of life and/or shorten the lifespan of a patient. The reasons that care is overprovided include financial incentives of health care providers, habit and the desires and preferences of patients. There is a proper role for patient preference and some patients will think the chance of a recovery or improvement given a medical reality will be worth it while others will not. What we need to do is learn to talk about this in a more open fashion and to expect that better information will be available to guide patient choices and decisions.

The extremely politicized nature of health policy in the United States harms our ability to discuss the need to improve the quality of health care. During the 2009–2010 health reform discussion, it seemed that many politicians felt they need to preface anything they said with the proviso "that we have the greatest health care system in the world." Anyone who dared to suggest this might not be the case, or that there were things that might be improved upon, were often roundly criticized then for somehow not loving America. This silly rhetoric has served to make it even harder for our nation to address quality problems in our current system. Improving the quality of health care as we seek to slow the rate of cost inflation is a priority.

I believe that health care expenditures should either improve quality of life and/or extend lifespan. You then need to know how much these improvements cost to judge whether they are worth it or not, a judgment with many subjective aspects. These complicated questions and how our culture revolts from asking them are addressed in detail in Chap. 6, but there is enough evidence of spending that neither improves quality of life nor increases life span to suggest that we can greatly slow the rate of health care cost inflation while improving quality.

The next step is to look briefly at the Affordable Care Act—what did the passage of it do to address these interrelated problems of cost, coverage, and quality—and what further steps are needed?

Chapter 4
Health Reform: The Policy

The passage of the ACA on March 21, 2010 was notable for many reasons. It was the most consequential health policy change enacted since Medicare and Medicaid in 1965, and one of the most comprehensive pieces of social legislation ever. It provided a route from the current 16–17% of the population lacking health insurance to 5–6% who will remain uninsured in 2020. It fills in the gap between employer-based insurance provided as a benefit of employment and government programs for the poor and elderly with a mandate for individuals to purchase coverage if they are not otherwise insured.

The law will expand coverage via Medicaid expansions, but will also more than double the number of Americans who purchase their own health insurance policy (from around 14 million today to 32 million in 2020). It limits the heretofore unlimited tax preference provided to employer paid insurance since World War II by imposing a tax on high cost insurance policies that will be implemented in 2018, and includes a kitchen sink approach that will develop and test new institutions and models that could decrease cost while improving quality.

Just as notably, it was passed entirely with the votes of one political party—60 members of the Senate, 219 in the House of Representatives and signed by President Obama. There is no other example of such a consequential law being passed without some members of the opposition political party.

The partisan nature of the months-long debate and passage does not match the policy reality of the law, which has the intellectual fingerprints of both parties. However, it remains politically toxic 2 years after its passage, and opposition helped to fuel large Congressional gains for Republicans in 2010.

This chapter and the next aim to morph the policy and political realities of the ACA in a way that makes clear what the ACA achieved and what it did not. Most importantly, it sets the stage for identifying the barriers to achieving a sustainable health care system in Chap. 6, before laying out what I see as the best next steps for our nation to take in health reform in Chap. 7. It is crucial to get health reform correct since addressing health care costs is a necessary, but not a sufficient condition for achieving a long range balanced budget. Without a coherent and broadly accepted health reform strategy, we have no hope of a balanced budget.

D.H. Taylor, Jr., *Balancing the Budget is a Progressive Priority*,
SpringerBriefs in Political Science, DOI 10.1007/978-1-4614-3664-5_4,
© Springer Science+Business Media, LLC 2012

First Step, or Last?

As I watched President Obama address Congress on September 10, 2009 to make the case for moving ahead with health reform, I was thrilled that health policy was front and center, but had one massive cringe moment—when he said that many Presidents had talked about health care reform and failed to achieve success, but that he intended to be the last.

There will never be a last step in health reform.

We will constantly be tinkering with the health care system, in large part because the health care system of tomorrow will have to deal with innovations that are unknown today. And any large complicated law that reformed a large complicated health care system would inevitably have to be revisited. In this more realistic spirit, the ACA was a good step toward our nation developing a sustainable health care system, in large part because it was a step. It represents what could pass the House, the Senate, and be signed by the President at the time. If it is the last step taken, we will not have a sustainable health care system; if it is repealed fully, we will not have a sustainable health care system.

To achieve a sustainable health care system will require constant tinkering, and the next steps will be the hardest. The ACA is not the last word on health reform, but instead the first word of a 30–40 year period of discussion, implementation, changing and tweaking that will be required to develop a sustainable system. If we can manage to move forward from this base, we have a chance at addressing health care costs and having a balanced budget in the future. If we cannot, we do not.

The ACA does six main things.

First, it creates an individual mandate to buy health insurance.

Second, it reforms insurance laws to ban preexisting conditions and rescissions (cancellation of coverage after a person becomes ill).

Third, it sets up a framework for state-based markets in which individuals and small businesses can purchase private health insurance in a setting that provides information to consumers designed to enable them be better shoppers.

Fourth, it provides income-based subsidies to help those with incomes between $28,000 and $90,000 (in 2010 dollars) to purchase private insurance, and expands Medicaid to cover those with lower incomes. All told, around 32 million persons will be insured in 2020 who would otherwise be uninsured.

Fifth, it cuts planned Medicare spending and increases taxes to offset increased spending on expanded insurance.

Sixth, it employs a variety of strategies to slow the rate of health care cost inflation. Prime examples include a tax on high cost health insurance, the Independent Payment Advisory Board (IPAB), and a variety of pilot projects and experiments that amount to a "kitchen sink" approach.

Individual Mandate

There is no example of a nation that has achieved universal health insurance coverage without a mandate of some sort. There are three types of mandates: expansion of government insurance, such as Medicare or Medicaid; an employer mandate in which businesses are required to provide coverage or to pay a tax to finance coverage; an individual mandate in which the onus for obtaining coverage is placed on individuals, typically with income based premium support to assist lower-income persons in purchasing private insurance.

All of these approaches are currently used in the United States. The payroll taxes that fund Part A of the Medicare program (hospital insurance) are not voluntary; instead, you are mandated to pay them and in return you gain the right to insurance coverage when you reach age 65. Likewise, income taxes pay the majority of the costs of Medicare Part B (doctor insurance) and you certainly are mandated to pay income taxes. The ACA increased the number of persons who are eligible for Medicaid, the federal/state insurance program for persons whose incomes fall below a certain threshold (set at 133% of poverty in the ACA) which today already covers around 60–65 million persons.

The state of Massachusetts enacted a law in 2006 that mandated that individuals purchase health insurance if they were not otherwise covered and provided subsidy amounts based on individual's income to help them do so. Massachusetts has achieved coverage of around 97% of the state's population. In fact, the ACA is patterned after the Massachusetts plan since it used an individual mandate and set up insurance markets designed to enable consumers to make good choices in purchasing coverage. This law was the centerpiece policy achievement of Republican Governor Mitt Romney's time as Governor of Massachusetts, at least until he began running for the Republican nomination for President. This demonstrates the continued political toxicity of the ACA—the biggest barrier to Gov. Romney becoming the Republican nominee for President is what is generally understood to be his greatest policy achievement.

The state of Hawaii has had an employer mandate in place since the 1970s, which means that businesses must provide insurance coverage to all full-time employees and some part-time ones. This policy has achieved approximately 92% coverage. Even without an employer mandate, a job is the way that 160 million Americans receive health insurance. However, over time, the employment-insurance linkage has been breaking down, making it a less reliable source of coverage, certainly in a time with high unemployment.

Where did the employment-insurance link come from anyway? In short, it was a historical accident that has proven to be very consequential. During World War II, there were broad wage and price controls in the US economy as the nation's industrial output was harnessed for the war effort. Large corporations seeking ways to compete for employees constructed the idea of a benefit—something provided to employees in return for their labor that was not taxable as income. Congress amended the tax code making such premiums not taxable income, allowing employers to compete for employees with benefits without violating wage and price controls. This seemingly innocuous decision started in process the system that we have today.

The elderly are universally covered by government health insurance once they reach age 65. The poor are covered by a government program (Medicaid), with the definition of what constitutes poor differing by state. Most others receive health insurance as a benefit of employment (including dependents) or they are uninsured. Just 14 million persons (out of 308 million) purchase their own health insurance policy today.

While there is still a strong linkage between employment and health insurance, it is breaking down somewhat with the rise of contract workers and other settings that reduce the employment cost to providers. Thus, the problem of the uninsured has been growing with time and will continue to do so. It is not an accident that the two states that have passed state insurance mandates, one an employer and the other an individual mandate, have the highest rates of insurance coverage in the United States. If one of your goals is to expand rates of health insurance coverage, it will take a mandate of some sort.

Interestingly, the individual mandate is a policy that has traditionally been favored by Republican politicians. In fact, the primary Republican alternative to the Clinton plan in 1993–1994, the Chafee plan, was based on an individual mandate to purchase insurance, the development of an improved insurance market in which the otherwise uninsured could purchase cover and a modest Medicaid expansion. That general idea should sound familiar.

Seventeen years later, a plan that is based on an individual mandate to purchase insurance, setting up insurance markets to enable consumers to shop for insurance and a Medicaid expansion (that is much larger in terms of how far up the poverty level it goes), became the basis of President Obama's health reform and was described as a government takeover of the health care system and/or a Socialist plot. How did a basic approach to expanding insurance coverage go from being the Republican alternative to the Clinton plan to the clearest sign of the End of the Republic in less than two decades?

There are two basic explanations. One is that the Republican party changed profoundly from 1994 to 2009–2010 in terms of health care insurance reform, the other that they decided they were going to challenge and oppose any legislative initiatives of President Obama as the best means of regaining power. Either explanation is bad news for moving ahead with a comprehensive health reform that includes insurance expansions.

Insurance Reform to Ban Denial of Coverage for Preexisting Conditions

The insurance reforms that ban preexisting conditions are as popular as the individual mandate to purchase insurance coverage is unpopular. The only thing I can think of that is worse than the status quo of the US health care system is eliminating the individual mandate while keeping the insurance coverage reforms, without adding some other means of pooling risks and reducing adverse selection. It seems an obvious fix: get rid of the unpopular individual mandate but keep the popular insurance market revisions. This is like telling your kids they can skip the vegetables, don't need to exercise, only have dessert and play video games, yet still be fit and trim.

If you get rid of the individual mandate but retain a ban on denial of insurance due to pre-existing conditions, then you will have persons who are sick sign up but fewer persons who are young and healthy. A legitimate worry about the ACA is whether the individual mandate is strong enough; I think it isn't and needs to be made more stringent to reduce adverse selection worries of this type. But, the insurance reforms go hand in hand with the individual mandate (or some type of mandate which is nothing more than a mechanism through which to pool insurance risks).

Setting Up State-Based Insurance Markets

The most radical aspect of ACA is the notion that individuals will shop for their own health insurance. The big idea is that competition for customers will cause insurance companies to compete, giving consumers more options and lower priced insurance. This idea is quintessentially American, but extremely rare when it comes to health insurance. In 2009, around 14 million Americans purchased their own health insurance policy meaning they applied for coverage, went through underwriting, were approved for a policy, and then paid their own premiums. In contrast, around 110 million persons had government-provided health insurance in the form of Medicare, Medicaid, or the Veterans Administration. According to the CBO, in 2020 there will be 32 million persons purchasing their own insurance through the health insurance markets that each state will set up, called exchanges.

These exchanges are based on the Massachusetts model whereby the state created websites that allowed consumers to compare policies based on monthly premium, out of pocket cost share when care is used, and the network of providers that are covered by a given policy (and therefore where you can receive care; what doctors and hospitals). A key aspect of both what was done in Massachusetts as well as what was passed in ACA is the development of standards regarding what types of care are covered by a given policy. States are granted large discretion in doing so.

While some lament the regulation inherent in this approach, without setting the basic definition of what type of care is covered, and what providers can be used, it renders comparison of plans based on monthly premium and cost share not meaningful. With no regulation, policies could differ fundamentally in what type of care is covered (such as not covering maternity care or mental health for example) making comparison shopping far more difficult. Persons in such cases could pick a low cost premium but find themselves not covered when they actually need coverage. One can of course say that they should be better shoppers, but especially if you are trying to get younger persons to get coverage, that is a strategy that will lead to predictably bad results. This is a bad idea, especially if society is unwilling to say "sorry you do not get care" to someone who chooses poorly.

A good deal of the success or failure of health reform will be how well states implement the insurance regulations and set up markets and whether these markets work well. States are given a great deal of latitude in setting up exchanges and some states are moving ahead with development of exchange policies while other states remain in full opposition mode and are not moving toward implementation. Some states that are dominated by Republicans are doing both, loudly protesting the ACA while moving to set up the infrastructure and policies needed to develop insurance exchanges by 2014. There are really two aspects to this process. The first is determining what standards and policies that states wish to mandate. The second, and likely most important, is determining how to communicate the complicated information inherent with purchasing health insurance to consumers in a meaningful manner that leads to informed choices.

Medicaid Expansions

In 2020, 32 million persons will have health insurance who otherwise will be uninsured. Half of these persons will be covered by Medicaid, the state/federal insurance program for persons with relatively low incomes. The ACA mandated that Medicaid covers all persons in families up to 133% of the federal poverty level (around $28,000 for a family of four). For some states, this represents a tremendous expansion of Medicaid coverage, while others had more expansive coverage standards of their own volition (since Medicaid provides minimum coverage levels but allows states to do more).

There are several issues that are worth noting in regard to using Medicaid as a coverage expansion approach. First, the reason it is an attractive means of expanding insurance coverage is that it is a straightforward means of doing so that can be controlled by simply increasing the income cutoff for eligibility. Second, the cost of financing Medicaid is shared between the federal and state government in question, with the rate of cost share determined by the relative wealth of the state. The default is for the state to pay half the cost of Medicaid, with more impoverished states paying a smaller proportion. For example, North Carolina pays around one-third of its Medicaid costs, and Mississippi pays around 18%, with the federal government paying the balance. The federal government will pay all of the extra costs for the Medicaid expansion through 2020. However, after that time the state cost share will be expected to revert to the common cost share. Third, Medicaid pays much lower rates to physicians and hospitals which leads to some cost shifting as well as difficulty for some beneficiaries to find providers willing to treat them. Further, a program that is known to be "insurance for poor people" is not very attractive, politically, and beneficiaries often face problems finding physicians who will treat them.

The reason it is so difficult to get persons with low income insured is that health insurance is expensive. If the 16 million persons who will be newly covered by Medicaid under the ACA were instead provided with premium support to purchase private insurance, it would be more expensive.

Cut Planned Medicare Spending to Partially Finance Insurance Expansions

There are only two ways to offset spending increases to expand insurance coverage: increase taxes or cut planned spending. The ACA does both. To finance insurance expansions, the law increases certain taxes and reduces planned Medicare payment increases over the same time period.

There are three main areas in which future Medicare spending will be cut by ACA. The first is a reduction in Disproportionate Share (DSH) payments to hospitals that are pro-rated based on how many uninsured patients a hospital cares for. It seems perfectly reasonable for DSH payments to drop given the expansion of insurance coverage.

Second, payments to Medicare Advantage plans are reduced to more typical levels (on a historical basis). Medicare Advantage are private insurance plans in which Medicare beneficiaries choose to enroll in HMOs, with Medicare paying a monthly premium that is based on the historical payment level in a beneficiary's county of residence. Historically, Medicare Advantage plans were paid 95% of the average adjusted per capita cost of all Medicare beneficiaries in a given plan. When established in the late 1970s and continued for the next 30 years, the plans were designed to save Medicare money based on the notion that the premium paid is 95% of the average cost to Medicare of caring for persons. However, cost savings have never materialized because the Medicare beneficiaries who have chosen to sign up for such plans have systematically been healthier than average. It has never been clear whether this effect has been entirely due to selection (only healthier beneficiaries are willing to take a more limited choice of providers) or whether private insurance companies have simply been able to market plans to healthier beneficiaries.

Payments to Medicare Advantage plans were greatly increased in 2005, as the Bush Administration and the Republican Congress sought to expand the "private" Medicare option. In some cases, Medicare advantage paid private insurance companies 114% of the average adjusted per capita cost in a county to pay for a beneficiary who choose such a plan. Around one in five Medicare beneficiaries are now enrolled in such plans.

Third, payment increases paid to certain types of providers (disproportionately home health) are to be less than they were set to be prior to the passage of the law.

Some have questioned whether it is legitimate or reasonable to use cuts in planned Medicare expenditures to fund insurance expansions for younger persons. I think the answer is yes, for several reasons. First, the Medicare program is large, thus making it a prime source of expenditure cuts. Second, there is a disconnect in the logic that states that Medicare spending is sacrosanct and shouldn't be cut to pay for insurance for younger persons. The younger persons who are having insurance financed at least partly via cuts to planned Medicare expenditures are the children, grandchildren, and great grandchildren of the Medicare beneficiaries in question. And these are the same persons who are and will pay the payroll taxes to fund Part A and income taxes to fund the general fund portion of Part B payments.

Increase Taxes to Partially Expand Insurance Expansions

A variety of taxes are increased by the ACA to partially pay for insurance expansions provided for in the ACA. These taxes fall into five major categories.

Taxes imposed on persons who do not comply with the individual mandate, and who remain uninsured. The tax penalty could range from $695 per year up to $2,085 per year, depending upon the household income of the person not complying (with higher incomes being taxed more).

An increase of 0.9% in the Medicare part A payroll tax for wages above $200,000 for individuals and $250,000 for couples.

A 3.8% tax on unearned income high wage earners ($200,000 for individuals, $250,000 couples).

An excise tax on high cost insurance policies. The tax of 40% will be applied to the value of policies above the following thresholds $10,200 for individuals, $27,500 for family policies, with the value of policies determined by the premiums paid by employers, as well as employer contributions to Flexible Savings accounts and other tax preferenced health care purchasing accounts. These levels will be indexed to overall inflation, so more policies will face these taxes over time if health care costs continue to rise much faster than inflation (which they will).

A variety of health care industry taxes that are denominated in dollar terms by industry and year, to be prorated to companies based on market share. Industries taxed include pharmaceuticals, the health insurance industry, medical device makers, and a 10% excise tax on indoor tanning salon services.

Aspects of ACA That Could Address Health Care Cost Inflation

Cost is one of the primary problems facing the US health care system, and more specifically, how much faster health care cost inflation is compared to overall inflation. The law has several aspects that can address and slow cost inflation if they are implemented as planned.

Tax on High Cost Insurance

The tax on high cost health insurance noted above is one of the most consequential changes in the ACA because it represents a de facto capping of the subsidy provided in the tax code to employer provided health insurance. This represents a profound change of the health insurance landscape of the past 60 years, and the President and the Democratic Congress have gotten too little credit in taking this step.

As described earlier, this tax expenditure is one of the largest in our tax code and amounts to a subsidy of around $250 billion last year that flowed to persons with employer provided health insurance, with high wage workers tending to receive the largest subsidy since those with higher wages tend to have more generous benefits. The imposition of the excise tax of 40% on the amount above target cap levels would create an incentive for insurance companies and employers to arrange for less generous benefits for their employees.

Altering the tax treatment of employer paid insurance is an obvious "next step" among policy wonks that would be taken to address health care costs. Indeed, this is another example of an idea that is typically associated with Republican health plans actually making it into the ACA. For example, then-Senator McCain's health plan in the 2008 Presidential campaign had at its center removing the tax preference of employer provided health insurance. Candidate Obama criticized this approach during the campaign, but the ACA contains a tax on high cost health insurance that will achieve at least a capping of this subsidy.

The tax on high cost insurance works in a roundabout way to achieve this goal. The rhetoric used in arguing for the tax focused on taxing insurance companies. However, such a tax will certainly be passed on to employers and therefore employees, since benefit costs are simply a portion of total compensation. This tax is one that is designed to be avoided, meaning the successful functioning of the tax will be shown through the reduction in generosity of benefit packages such that new total premium amounts will be below the level at which the tax applies. For employees, it is designed to trigger a conversation between employer and employee in which health insurance benefits are explicitly discussed as a portion of total employment costs. Employees who now receive benefits and who may not even know their value will be incentivized to know in the future. This will shift some compensation from tax free (employer paid premiums) to taxable wages, increasing tax receipts.

Reforming the tax treatment of employer paid insurance will put downward pressure on cost inflation in the private insurance market. It is important to address costs in both private insurance and Medicare since payment differentials that are too large will likely proved to be very dislocating to the ability of Medicare beneficiaries to access health care services. We must address cost inflation in the private insurance market as well as in Medicare, and the tax on high cost health insurance is a start to doing so.

The Independent Payment Advisory Board

For the Medicare program, the Independent Payment Advisory Board is a means of slowing health care cost inflation. However, this board has also been perhaps the most politically toxic aspect of the law save the individual mandate. The board is based broadly on the concept of the Base Realignment Commission (BRAC), more commonly known as the base closing commission that was successfully used on two occasions to undertake the politically difficult decision to close military bases.

Because such bases are key economic lifelines in local communities, the mere suggestion of closing a base would result in ferocious political opposition. Even people, who believe that in the abstract we have too many military bases, do not believe the one in their town, or in their Congressional district, should be closed. The point of such a board is to give experts the authority to make hard decisions in a manner that is insulated politically. In the case of the BRAC, Congress had to vote the entirety of the board's recommendations up or down.

The IPAB is a similarly designed board experts who would make recommendations for how to change Medicare payment policies if health care costs grew too rapidly; any recommendations from IPAB would likewise have to be voted up or down by Congress. The President would nominate members of the board and the Senate would confirm them. Once in place, the recommendations of the IPAB would become binding unless Congress overrode them in their entirety for a given year.

The IPAB has been a flash point for the discussion of rationing during the debate of the ACA and in the aftermath. Most of this discussion has not been based in the actual reality of the policy mechanisms available to the IPAB, and the repeal of IPAB has become a top level target by Republican politicians as well as for some Democrats. A fuller discussion of the IPAB and how I believe this board should be strengthened is provided in Chap. 7. Here are several facts about the IPAB as passed in the ACA:

Members who are appointed are expected to leave their job and undertake work on the IPAB as their full time employment. This has raised concerns about the willingness of the best persons to serve on the board.

Certain Medicare providers and types of care are exempted from IPAB jurisdiction for the first 10 years of the law, most notably hospitals. This will limit the scope of the board in the near term.

The IPAB will only be called upon to issue recommendations that will become binding if health care costs increase above a certain rate. Recently, CBO projected that this standard was not likely to be met in the first 10 years of the ACA, which if true would mean that no IPAB-based savings could be projected. The reason this is important is that it would allow for Congress to repeal the IPAB section of the ACA without having to identify funding offsets that would allow them to say they had not increased the budget deficit.

The IPAB is explicitly forbidden from making coverage decisions or from rationing of health care services in the ACA, as defined in the statute as follows in subsection (c)(2), the ACA says:

> (ii) The proposal shall not include any recommendation to ration health care, raise revenues or Medicare beneficiary premiums under section 1818, 1818A, or 1839, increase Medicare beneficiary cost sharing (including deductibles, coinsurance, and copayments), or otherwise restrict benefits or modify eligibility criteria. (42 USC 1899A(c)(2)(ii)).

The work of the IPAB will likely be subject to much litigation, especially as sellers and providers of health care services who could have their Medicare-based income streams disrupted seek all options to avoid this outcome.

President Obama in March of 2011 actually pledged to strengthen the IPAB, making the standard that would require IPAB recommendations to be lower, and to strengthen the ability of IPAB to improve quality of care.

Medicare Innovation Center, Etc.

The ACA contains a veritable "kitchen sink" of pilot programs and tests and ideas that could lead to improvements in how care is provided and paid for, hopefully leading to improved quality and perhaps reduced cost. Basically, many promising ideas are included in the law, which has led some to deride the scattershot approach. However, we have known for a long time that there are many fundamental problems with how health care is paid for in the Medicare program. Most notably, a fee for service-based approach incentives and rewards hospitals and providers for having patients who are ill and use lots of care. The ACA finally produces a route to experimentation actually changing and improving Medicare policy. We need to try everything, and changes in the Medicare program have historically filtered down into private health insurance, so Medicare is an appropriate place to test new models of care.

One of the negative aspects of the continued political environment related to health reform is that any new idea that does not pan out or work as intended is taken as a "gotcha" moment that is used politically to invalidate the entire ACA. This is one of the reasons that we desperately need a political agreement to make health reform the vehicle of both political parties. Of course some things will not work, of course there will be unintended consequences that must be addressed and tweaked. There are always unintended consequences and we need to get to the point in which we are able to use the results of experiments and demonstrations to move ahead, whether they work as intended or not.

The biggest hindrance to using new information—both things that work as well as things that fail—to inform our next steps in health reform is the fact that the ACA remains embroiled in a political firestorm. Every new finding is first and foremost fodder in the ongoing political war surrounding the ACA. That must stop if we are ever going to have a balanced budget.

Chapter 5
Health Reform: The Politics

I was in Washington, DC with my two sons (then 9 and 13) the weekend of March 19–21, 2010. As we emerged from the Union Station Metro stop that bright Saturday morning, I got goose bumps when I saw the Capitol Dome, in part because I like public spaces, but also because it was a momentous weekend. That day, the House began debating the final passage of the Senate bill as well as the reconciliation bill that paved the way for final passage of the Affordable Care Act (ACA) that was signed into law on March 23, 2010.

We got a chance to watch some of the debate from the House gallery, and I was as intent as my sons were bored: my 9 year old won the day with a tug of my shirt, and his clear preference that we leave the "boring talking" to go and ride the airplane simulator in the Smithsonian that lets you "flip upside down until you nearly puke."

As we walked from the Capitol to the Smithsonian, my sons got a very practical introduction to a key American value: dissent and protest. We waded into the middle of the anti-health reform protest and listened to a bit of it, taking in the scene. "Dad, there are a lot of mad old people here," was my 9 year old's take. However, I noticed more families with younger and adolescent kids of my children's age than I would have predicted. And the most vivid image of protest for me is a kid of about 10 chanting "Kill the Bill" over and over inside a Metro stop later in the day.

As we travelled home at the end of the weekend, I was sure that the passage of the ACA would lessen the vehemence of the protests and that the country would settle into the implementation of the new law. Boy was I wrong.

The passage of the ACA became the rallying cry of the Republican party, and more directly for the Tea Party wing of the Republican party (and like-minded Independents as well), fueling their 2010 election campaign. The passage of the law became a symbol of the federal government overstepping its Constitutionally prescribed bounds of power and control of the House of Representatives changed from Democratic to Republican and Republicans made large gains in the Senate.

I never got the vehemence of the political opposition to the law, because I viewed the ACA in policy terms. President Obama and Congressional Democrats embraced an individual mandate and the creation of private insurance markets (and a Medicaid expansion) to move us closer to universal coverage, not a Medicare-for-all proposal favored by many Liberals. An individual mandate had been the preferred route for Conservatives interested in expanding health insurance coverage since the early 1990s when Mark Pauly and others published a short book called *Responsible National Health Insurance*. The third principle of the plan was that "All citizens should be required to obtain a basic level of health insurance." In the debate over the Clinton Health Reform Plan a few years later, the so-called Chaffee plan became the primary Republican alternative that relied on an individual mandate and the setting up of insurance markets to aid consumers in making their purchasing decisions.

Phrases often used by Conservatives arguing for an individual mandate in the past included: responsibility, common sense, efficiency, and fairness. Phrases used by many of the same people to describe the individual mandate once it became central to the ACA: unconstitutional, heavy handed, unfair, and socialism. A February 16, 2010 story on NPR chronicled the intellectual and political history of the individual mandate and the irony that once adopted by the Democratic party it became unpalatable to Conservatives. The list of notable Republicans that supported the individual mandate as the responsible way to expand insurance coverage, who later changed their minds, is not short: Grassley, Dole, Hatch, Gingrich, Bennett, McCain, and many more.

When viewed in policy terms, the Democratic party appears to have negotiated with itself in the passage of the ACA, and developed a plan that is similar to what might have been expected to arise had the parties actually negotiated a bipartisan reform deal. Why did a plan that was moderate and bipartisan in policy terms become so politically potent for Republicans that none of them voted for a bill that had at its heart ideas long espoused by them?

I think it boils down to a Rorschach test of sorts: President Obama and Congressional Democrats froze out and didn't allow Republicans access to the negotiations that developed the law;

Or

Republicans were going to vote against anything supported by President Obama, because they were committed to nothing as strongly as they were to his political defeat.

Half the country thinks it is the first, and the other half thinks it is the second. For me, in the end, most Republicans seem to be reflexively opposed to anything that President Obama is for and they simply had to try and deny him a victory in health reform.

Political Flashpoints: Individual Mandate and Rationing

The rhetoric used against the individual mandate has provided the political space in which the Supreme Court could plausibly rule the individual mandate to be unconstitutional when the hear the case during their 2012 term. This outcome would have seemed absurd during the Summer of 2009 as House committees began reporting out early versions of the bills that ultimately became the ACA.

As late as June 14, 2009, Senator Charles Grassley (R-Iowa), the ranking Minority member of the key Senate Finance Committee, stated that there was a bipartisan agreement that an individual mandate was the best way to increase insurance coverage. Senator Grassley was not only the leading Republican on the Senate Finance Committee; he was one of the "gang of six" from this committee who were said to be negotiating compromise legislation from July–September, 2009. However, by October 2009 Senator Grassley was not only against the version of the ACA that was passed by the Senate finance committee (with one Republican vote, Olympia Snowe of Maine), he flatly said that the presence of an individual mandate in any reform law was a deal breaker.

Senator Grassley also infamously noted during town hall meetings in August 2009 that we shouldn't be "pulling the plug on grandma" as the presence of expanded reimbursement for palliative care consultation within Medicare as proposed in the bill had come to be called "death panels." Of course, Senator Grassley had previously supported expanded access for palliative care, and he knew that there was nothing remotely close to "pulling the plug on grandma" in the ACA. Senator Grassley certainly wasn't the only Republican politician who raised the specter of rationing for political expediency in their fight against the ACA, he was, however, a member of the Senate who was involved in negotiations about the details of the law and knew better. However, in the drive against the ACA, nothing seemed to be out of bounds.

Politicians can of course change their mind. It seem as though Republicans changed theirs about the individual mandate only as it appeared that a major step ahead on health reform was about to take place, which of course would give President Obama and the Democratic Party a major victory. If Republicans would have joined in, they could have improved the law and advanced long-term interests of theirs such as medical malpractice reform and together the two parties may have done much more to address health care cost inflation. Perhaps the delayed tax on high cost health insurance could have been a more straightforward capping of the tax preference afforded to employer provided insurance.

Republican members of Congress will of course say they were frozen out of the process. However, after the election of Scott Brown to the Massachusetts Senate seat vacated by Ted Kennedy's death rid Democrats of the 60 votes they needed to override a filibuster in the Senate, one Republican Senator could have gotten quite a lot to simply vote for a motion to proceed to consider a conference committee bill on the ACA. Three or four working together could have gotten almost anything. Then they could have shared the victory, but the notion of shared political victories did not abound in the 111th Congress.

The Patients' Choice Act

One of the leading candidates for the Republican Presidential nomination in 2012, Mitt Romney, presided over the passing of an individual mandate-based reform plan that has pushed the rate of insurance to around 97% in that state showing that the Republican party's fealty to the individual mandate was not only theoretical.

Even more proximate to the debate around the ACA, the 111th Congress saw the introduction of the Patients' Choice Act (PCA), cosponsored by Senators Tom Coburn (R-Oklahoma) and Richard Burr (R-North Carolina) and House members Paul Ryan (R-Wisconsin) and Devin Nunes (R-California). This bill was introduced on May 20, 2009, around 1 month before the first of the Democratically controlled House committees reported out early versions of HR 3200, the House version of the reform bill.

This Republican-sponsored bill is fascinating because of its use of soft individual mandates and the introduction of two boards to apply cost effectiveness research and guidelines broadly in the health care system that are similar to the Independent Payment Advisory Board (IPAB)—the two most potent political symbols of Republican opposition to the ACA. In short, they were great ideas when proposed by Republicans but foretold the end of the Republic when proposed by Democrats.

The PCA aimed to set up state-based insurance markets in which individuals could purchase private insurance. The bill was never scored by the CBO (and still hasn't been as of January 2012), and while a fairly comprehensive proposal, there were many details that were not made plain in the text, which would have had to be fleshed out had it come under serious consideration (committee hearings, bill mark ups, and the like). Following is a brief review in the ways that the ACA adopted ideas that initially appeared in the most comprehensive Republican-sponsored reform bill introduced into the 111th Congress, the Patients' Choice Act.

Soft Individual Mandates

The PCA foresaw a series of soft individual mandates designed to get persons to sign up for insurance. Examples included auto-enroll procedures when persons did things like sign up for or renew a drivers license. If uninsured, someone renewing a drivers license would be auto-enrolled in the most basic catastrophic plan unless he or she explicitly opted out. A staffer for one of the sponsors of the Patients Choice Act talked with me about the need for some sort of mandate to get persons covered during the Summer of 2009, explaining that if you didn't get a broad cross-section of the public signed up for such insurance, that you would run the risk of adverse selection blowing up the risk pool. That is why you have an individual mandate. Given that the penalty proscribed in the ACA for violating the individual mandate and not signing up is quite weak, the practical difference between the degree to which the PCA and the ACA mandated persons into health insurance is unclear.

The Patients' Choice Act 47

It would have of course depended upon what a more final version of the PCA would have looked like. However, the policy staffers of the sponsors knew they had to have a way to compel people into insurance for this approach to work. You certainly wouldn't know that from the political rhetoric in opposition to the individual mandate in the ACA.

End Tax Exclusion of Employer Paid Insurance

This is the most consequential aspect of the proposed PCA from a cost perspective. The bill, like the proposal made by Senator McCain during the Presidential campaign, would completely end the preferential tax treatment of employer paid insurance, undoing a subsidy that has quietly helped to encourage employer-based insurance since World War II. It has also shielded persons receiving employer-based coverage from the true cost of their health insurance. This is easily the best next step to address health care cost inflation in the private market and I embrace it.

Under the PCA, each person would receive a tax credit that could be used to purchase private health insurance. Essentially this would redistribute the tax preference that currently benefits those with expansive employer based coverage, and equalize the subsidy so that everyone would get the same amount in the form of a tax credit with which to purchase health insurance. This policy would result in a very large redistribution of benefit from those with excellent employer-based coverage to those who were uninsured, or who were self-employed and therefore didn't fully benefit from the way the tax code now preferences employer-based insurance.

Republicans have long talked about reforming the tax treatment of employer paid health insurance, but the Democrats actually did it via the tax on high cost health insurance (delayed until 2018 in the reconciliation bill). If Republicans had acknowledged the ACA as a cousin to the PCA they could have exerted some influence on it, and perhaps a more direct capping of the subsidy would have resulted.

Tax Credit Would Provide Catastrophic Coverage Only

Unstated in the PCA and in the rhetoric of the proponents, the amount of tax credit could purchase a catastrophic insurance policy only. The value of the family tax credit proposed was $5,900 in 2009, while the average cost of a family policy in the United States that year was $13,500. There is nothing wrong with proposing catastrophic insurance, but the sponsors of the bill never made clear that is all that could be financed with the magnitude of the tax credit proposed. Further, even the modest value of the proposed tax credit would not be fully offset in cost terms by ending the tax preference of employer provided insurance, so another source of revenue would have been required to make the PCA pass muster with the standard that a bill not increase the deficit over 10 years time.

Proposed Board of Experts to Make Policy Decisions for the Entire Health Care System

The PCA proposed setting up two federal boards that were insulated from the work of Congress to apply cost effectiveness research, practice guidelines and quality standards across the entire health care system. Their withering criticism of the Independent Payment Advisory Board (IPAB) in the ACA suggests that Democrats dreamed up this idea, but the general idea was first suggested in the 111th Congress by the PCA.

Title VIII (pp. 205–216 of the bill) of the PCA set up an expert advisory board to apply cost effectiveness research to medical treatment decision making, and which granted the board powers to bar physicians not following such rules and guidelines from billing governmental insurance programs such as Medicare and Medicaid. This means that 1 month before the first bill was passed out of a House Committee, a Republican bill envisioned a board that would be tasked with applying cost effectiveness research and the use of guidelines throughout the health care system (not just in Medicare), and that had a more powerful ultimate penalty than what actually was created by the ACA, the IPAB (the IPAB can merely enact payment changes, while the PCA board could ban providers from billing Medicare or Medicaid if they didn't follow guidelines). The inclusion of the IPAB in the ACA is an example of an idea first suggested by Republicans making it into the final health reform legislation, but that does not stop the criticism of the IPAB from continuing to be apocalyptic.

When proposed in the PCA, boards made up of experts appointed by the President and confirmed by the Senate were a good way to bring expertise to bear on the health care system, but when a similar board was put into the ACA, it was a rationing board populated by bureaucrats who want to kill your grandmother.

Cake Not Fully Cooked

One argument that was made in favor of the PCA was that it was much shorter than the ACA, and the PCA was only 260 pages long as introduced. However, part of the reason it was shorter was because it wasn't finished, meaning there were numerous statements that would have had to be fleshed out into legislative language if the Act were to be considered for passage into law. An example follows.

Tax credits provided to people to purchase insurance in the PCA could be used to buy policies sold in the state-based Health Insurance Exchanges, but they could also be used to purchase policies sold outside of the exchanges. However, only policies sold inside the exchanges would ban the use of preexisting conditions to either deny or underwrite health insurance policies. Thus, there would be a danger that only the sickest patients would seek coverage via the exchange, since coverage in exchanges cannot be denied. Outside the exchanges, policies could be denied, so healthier patients could likely get a better price outside exchanges. If this happened systematically, it could result in death spiral whereby only poor risks are included in exchange-based plans. However, the text of the PCA (sec 202 (d), pp. 22–25 of the bill) notes that exchanges "shall develop mechanisms to protect enrollees from the imposition of excessive premiums, reduce adverse selection, and share risk." The legislative language and/or the rules and regulations required to translate that simple clause into reality would be many, many pages long. So, part of the reason that the PCA was short is that it was not a finished product.

The Political Bottom Line

I coach my 10 year olds little league football team and have come to know that defense is easier than offense. On offense, one player can make a mistake and the perfect execution of ten others is rendered useless. On defense, it is exactly the opposite, and one defender can sack the quarterback even if his teammates fail in their assignment. The Republican Party has shown itself to be expert at arguing against health reform proposals using strident, ideological language. This remains true in the debate around the ACA even though many of the basic policy initiatives at the heart of the law are ideas that either came from Republicans or were not incongruent with their health policy approach until they showed up in the ACA.

The primary political themes of opposition to the ACA were limits of freedom in the form of the individual mandate, and fear of death as a result of rationing, as encapsulated in opposition to the IPAB. The switch on the individual mandate seems to be simple political opportunism to me. The rationing line of attack on the IPAB is a tried and true strategy that Republicans have perfected to an art form.

However, there is a bipartisan dimension to using fear to argue against your opponent's health reform plan. In the end, the bottom line message of some Republicans arguing against the IPAB and of some Democrats arguing against Rep. Paul Ryan's April 2011 plan to transition Medicare to a program in which seniors will purchase private health insurance using vouchers is simple: the other side wants to kill your grandma. This line of attack is very effective in playing upon the fear of death and the inability to face the concept of limits in medicine that is pervasive in our culture. It is easier to deconstruct the other side's arguments than it is to propose something better. Our culture enables and incentivizes this line of political attack, and that is the biggest barrier to our developing a sustainable health care system.

Chapter 6
Health Reform: The Barriers

It is our cultural fear of death and inability to discuss the limits of medicine to forestall death that enables the politics of health reform to be so potent.

When I did a postdoctoral fellowship in England in the mid-1990s, a professor I met who had lived in the United States explained to me why he thought health policy discussions in that nation were so much more honest and straightforward than were those in the United States. The UK, he explained, was a country that believed reflexively in Original Sin, regardless of what an individual's religious beliefs might be. They were not surprised when things were bad, and they fully expected them to get worse! This general perspective held true he said for the weather, how England would do in the World Cup as well as in health policy. So, the English people weren't surprised by waits for some medical procedures, for example, and preferred an honest discussion on how to make them as short as possible, to pretending that limits to what the NHS could afford to spend on health care did not exist.

In the United States, he surmised, we believe in the perfectibility of humankind, again reflexively and without respect to religious views. This means that we assume that with enough effort, energy, and focus we can fix anything. This of course runs counter to what I have termed the first law of health care systems: that everyone dies.

That everyone dies doesn't mean that we shouldn't attempt to prevent and treat illness, but that inevitably, we reach diminishing returns on the health care investments we make to forestall death. It can be quite difficult to determine when this occurs, and harder still to decide what to do about it. However, in the United States, we do not seem to even be able to ask the question that flows naturally from diminishing returns: is this procedure worth it?

Of course the answer is laden with many value judgments. But not asking the question too has values, and means that we often spend substantial sums of money on care that may actually shorten lifespan and reduce quality of life, in the miniscule chance of achieving a miracle. Our expectation that we should be able to conquer any disease if we just work hard enough hinders our ability to have honest, open, and realistic conversations about the existence of limits in what medicine can do.

D.H. Taylor, Jr., *Balancing the Budget is a Progressive Priority*,
SpringerBriefs in Political Science, DOI 10.1007/978-1-4614-3664-5_6,
© Springer Science+Business Media, LLC 2012

It is our culture's inability to honestly wrestle with these limits, and practically coming to grips with the reality that everyone eventually dies, that is the root cause of why our health system is unsustainable.

Beginning to face this reality and ask the question "is it worth it?" is the only way we can address health care costs and transition to a sustainable system.

We Have to Develop Our Own System

I don't use the example of the NHS to now launch into an argument for why we should copy their health care system. Quite the opposite. We couldn't copy it even if we wanted to do so (and I do not in any event) because it exists in a cultural and historical context. It was created by the people of England for the people of England. I do think it is interesting and can be informative to look at what other nations do and do not do in the area of health care. Cross-national comparisons do provide a menu of options and help to show that we are not getting our money's worth from what we spend on health care in the United States, but they don't self-evidently direct our reform efforts. Talk of copying another nation's health system is both a bad idea and a waste of time.

We have to develop a health care system that is sustainable and works for our nation, created by us, for us.

In order to do so, we must first learn how to talk about limits, and to acknowledge the inevitability of diminishing returns. Even with advances in therapies, there will still inevitably be a point of diminishing returns, so long as everyone eventually dies. The next breakthrough simply produces more questions about when it should be applied.

We must not only talk about these issues in a cultural sense, but begin to translate discussions into policies that can identify when returns are diminishing beyond a level at which we are willing to spend given the expected benefits. It will not be easy to achieve a system based on an honest acknowledgment of limits. It will require hard work, given the gulf between our stated views about the need to control costs and our cultural default to assume that more is always better in health care. And it is not a one-way street in which we first talk and then institute policies. The only way we will actually talk is to begin to implement policies that could begin to slow the rate of health care cost inflation in our system.

We have no hope of ever having a balanced budget without addressing health care costs. And we have little hope of doing this without learning how to talk about limits.

The Biggest Obstacle Is Us

The biggest obstacle to addressing health care costs is not technical: it is us. Over the past couple of years, I have had the privilege of talking with a variety of community groups about health care reform, the role of health care in our nation's budget woes, and my views of what the next steps after the ACA should be to move us toward a sustainable health care system. In giving talks like this, it is easy to show slides about rising costs and to elicit knowing nods that we must do something to slow down the rate of cost inflation. There is a common gut level understanding that our system is unsustainable and that we need to do *something* to address health care costs.

However, when I shift gears and talk about *anything* that has a chance of slowing the rate of cost inflation in health care, people change their mind. No, not that…that is not what we meant! We want the magic solution where we revolutionize our system to slow spending, but change nothing in the way of what is available, how provided and how much providers are paid for delivering it. My bottom line conclusion is that we as a people are profoundly delusional when it comes to health care. We say that we want to reduce "out of control spending," but we are opposed to any change that has a chance of resulting in the outcome we say we want.

Can Anyone Say No?

As I was first working on this book over the Christmas holidays of 2010, two examples of this disconnect were in the news. These examples are not unique, just on the front page of my local paper. Blue Cross Blue Shield of North Carolina (BCBS NC) announced a new set of rules that govern when they (largest insurer in North Carolina with around 70% of the market share) will pay for spinal fusion surgery. This is a surgical procedure that is designed to lessen lower back pain, which is a common chronic health condition that results in a great deal of suffering. There has long been uncertainty about the best way to treat low back pain, with expensive surgical interventions often having trouble demonstrating improvements over much less intensive interventions such as exercise, physical therapy, pharmaceuticals, and waiting. Many patients favor intensive treatments, even in the absence of clear evidence that they work any better, and they have more risks to boot. In this case, spinal fusion surgery is around three times as expensive as another surgical procedure, that is, in turn, more intensive than other common treatment options. The difference in outcomes of the options is unclear.

BCBS NC did not say they will never pay for spinal fusion surgery, but instead they are tightening the criteria for when they will do so to ensure that the procedure is warranted. In other words, under some circumstances they will say no, we will not pay for spinal fusion surgery. If we ever slow the rate of cost inflation in health care, there will be numerous instances like this—where we begin to spend less than we otherwise would have with no change. Someone will have to say no to something that is likely to be provided by default if we are going to slow the rate of health care spending increase. The possibilities of who could say no are patients and families, insurers, be they government or private, and health care providers. If there are not any changes in how these actors currently think about and act in making health care decisions, we will not address health care costs.

The reaction to BCBS NC's decision was predictable. The American Association of Neurological Surgeons and the North Carolina Spine Society lodged complaints against BCBS NC and their planned change. They professed worry about the welfare of their patients, and also linked this decision to the broader health reform context. "If this intrusion into the physician–patient relationship goes unchallenged, other insurers will follow" Dr. John Wilson a neurosurgeon at Wake Forest University is quoted as saying in the December 25, 2010 Raleigh, NC *News and Observer*. The use of this type of spinal surgery in the Medicare program is also controversial, and some say Medicare should review its criteria regarding when the procedure should be covered. The number of procedures paid for by Medicare has quintupled since its approval as a treatment option in 1997, and Medicare routinely covers nonexperimental therapies with almost no oversight so long as there is a willing patient and a ready provider.

Briefly, the arguments and interests in this case:

BCBS NC says the evidence that this procedure works is shaky, and wants to approve it in more limited cases, when other therapies have already been tried but not worked.

Physicians object on two grounds: this will harm their patients and the slippery slope argument that if an insurer gets between the doctor and the patient here it will further erode the doctor–patient relationship and further harm patients.

Unstated by the surgeon groups is that the procedure is lucrative for them.

Unstated by the insurance company is that denying the procedure reduces their outlays or payment for care, so is lucrative for them.

Patients are suffering from low back pain, and understandably want it fixed. It is a miserable condition and how it should be treated has long been a vexing problem, mostly because nothing seems to work well. The only way a procedure can expand fourfold in a little over a decade is for a lot of patients to assent to receiving the treatment. Obviously the average patient relies upon his or her doctor for advice, and if the surgeon says the procedure will help them, most are in no position to evaluate the evidence for the procedure and decide for themselves. And when in doubt, our culture assumes that more is better.

The state of the research seems to indicate that this procedure is not any better than other options. And it is three times more expensive than other surgical procedures; even if better, it is not three times better. When you factor in the risks, it could even be worse.

A key policy question is what the default: when in doubt cover everything, even in the absence of clear evidence that it works? Or, is the default to not cover something if the evidence of its benefit is not clear?

So, we are left with the public saying they want to put an end to "out of control health care spending" but most of these same individuals will decry the move by BCBS NC as rationing that is inappropriate. Any comment from the public will be disproportionately weighted toward outrage that an insurance company may not cover the procedure in certain circumstances. Persons without low back pain will not pay much attention, but those with the problem and advocates will decry the removal of a treatment option from some patients. And many will assume that BCBS NC and any other private insurance company are only out to reduce their payout for care as a way to improve their bottom line. They of course do have this as a motivation. And the most likely outcome is that a procedure that is not proven to be better than other therapies yet costs many times more will be provided and paid for by BCBS NC. Even if definitive research proof is found that the surgery is not worthwhile, such a technical answer is unlikely to prove persuasive without a change in how our culture talks about these sorts of issues.

And right on cue, 6 weeks after the initial story of BCBS NC's proposed change there was an announcement late in January 2011 that the policy had been modified after meeting with provider groups. Some applications of various surgical procedures were removed from the policy (for example, pediatric surgeries were removed from the policy and were instead to be decided on a case-by-case basis) and other changes were made, all having the effect of making it more likely that BCBS NC would pay for more surgeries. I do not know if this was a reasonable settlement of this dispute or not, but I know that the largest barrier to reducing health care spending is cultural acceptance that reducing spending means delivering less care. We say we want to save money, but anything that could do this will be met with the retort, "*that* is not what I meant."

This general story could be told with dozens of examples. It will be able to be told a decade from now for a therapy that has yet to be discovered.

Saying No to Palliative Care

Another example was in the *New York Times* the day after Christmas, 2010. Medicare announced that it would begin to pay for the following as a part of an annual physical: counseling of patients about end-of-life options available to them, such as living wills and advance directives, the availability of hospice care should they need and want it, and related matters. A provision in earlier versions of the ACA to create a separate benefit for such consultations in Medicare morphed politically into the infamous "death panels" in August 2009. Getting from increased payment so that patients and physicians could discuss options as they face their illness(es) into death panels was a preposterous "political misstatement" designed to defeat the bill. In December 2010, Medicare decided to implement the change via the regulatory process implemented by CMS, the agency in the executive branch that runs Medicare and Medicaid.

In early January 2011, CMS abruptly altered course, and dropped the regulation change that allowed for the reimbursement by Medicare of these services as part of a covered annual physical. The White House overrode the decision of CMS to bring about this change because of political concerns that the renewed charges of "death panels" being secretly put into Medicare. In fairness, there were questions about whether CMS followed the appropriate rules about public notice of changes in Medicare regulations, and this uncertainty meant that litigation of the items was assured. So, the decision to pull back from the rule was probably correct, perhaps on the technical merits of not following proper procedure, and certainly because it seemed sneaky to many.

However, the reticence to engage the conversation about how Medicare beneficiaries wish to be cared for as they become sicker and approach death tells us a great deal about our culture, and our inability to even fathom directly the concept of limits to what medicine can do, and diminishing returns for the continued use of aggressive therapy.

It is fascinating that one of the enduring images of health reform is a lie: "death panels." That expanded coverage of counseling to give patients information, options and inform them of their choices including palliative care became "death panel" is absurd and devoid of fact. However, the power of the charge and the entry of this phrase into our cultural vocabulary illustrate our cultural fear of not having access to the medicine-based miracle that we all seem to assume must exist. And the idea that a government insurance program (Medicare) would be the purveyor of something as ominous as being "sentenced to death" (again a lie) by a panel of bureaucrats makes the phrase all the scarier. However, as you can see from the BCBS NC example, having a private insurance company impose rules that could reduce the receipt of health care services doesn't make it any less explosive politically and culturally.

Interestingly, expanded access to palliative care consultation and discussion of end-of-life issues is a route to increasing access to care that has been shown to improve quality of life of patients with serious life-limiting illness. So, the bottom line effect of the strange "death panel" lie is to harm patients, the exact opposite of what those charging "death panels" claim to be interested in.

Hospice has long been shown to improve patient and family satisfaction and quality of life among patients who are believed to have less than 6 months to live and who decide to forgo aggressive care based on their wishes. Nearly half of all Medicare beneficiaries use some hospice prior to their death, up from less than 10% in 1990. In other words, hospice has passed the market test. And from family experience and talking with others, the typical take on hospice is that they enter people's lives at the most difficult time, and help people and their families in their hour of ultimate need. There is evidence that hospice actually reduces Medicare costs near death as compared to what they would be if patients used normal care, which often means dying in a hospital, the most expensive part of the health care system.

And access to palliative care—all care that focuses on improving quality of life regardless of prognosis—earlier rather than later in a terminal disease course has been shown to improve quality of life and even to extend lifespan in some studies (hospice is a subset of palliative care). In the year-end 2010 lists, many noted a randomized control trial showing that early palliative care for persons newly diagnosed with stage IV lung cancer improved quality of life, extended life, and actually reduced costs as one of the top medical articles of the year. Make no mistake; receiving a diagnosis of stage IV lung cancer is grave. However, in this study, those who received early access to palliative care lived an average of 12 months as compared to 9 months, had better quality of life, and lower health care costs.

Expanded access to discussing palliative care options is what was politically labeled as "death panels" during the health reform debate. The result was removing expanded funding to discuss options for such care from the ACA, which should best be understood to have denied patients access to care that could help them. Arguing for expanded access to palliative care remains politically toxic due to the strange "death panel" lie that began in August 2009 as a way to defeat the ACA.

On the other hand, the spinal fusion surgery is not proven to work any better than other available therapies, and costs a great deal more. So, expanded coverage of this procedure is exposing patients to an invasive and risky procedure that is far from proven to be worth it.

These two vignettes clearly demonstrate the cultural default in our nation when it comes to health care: when in doubt, do more. And when further discussing what should be done, assume that anything that argues for less intensive medical treatments is not only bad, but possibly evil. There is no technical answer to our health care cost problem that does not include hard choices, clear statements of values, and open and honest discussion of limits. Given that everyone dies, eventually you encounter diminishing returns in what is being done to forestall death. If you read this sentence and reflexively revolt, it means that deep down you think it is possible you could live forever. You cannot.

The only way to deal with the disconnect between statements that we must slow health care spending and revulsion against any policy that might plausibly achieve what we claim to want is to learn how to talk openly about limits in medicine and to then develop practical solutions that can slow the rate of cost inflation in health care. In developing a means doing so, we need to commit to developing an American way of doing it, that flows out of our culture and works in our culture. The hardest part of doing this will not be technical.

Focus on Value

What we most need to move the US health care system toward sustainability is a value revolution. By that I mean that we need to ask and bring focus to answering to the following three questions when considering health care for a patient:

Does it improve quality of life?
Does it extend the patient's life?
How much does it cost?

Only with an answer to these three questions can we begin to formulate an answer to the question "is it worth it?" I don't know how we should put these questions and the answers together to make decisions, but we (the 308 million person version) have to learn how to talk about this and decide how we will respond. It will be hard, and it will be scary. But, not doing so is also scary.

The *bad bad* news is that our health care system is on autopilot to bankrupt our country. The *good bad* news is that we are not getting our money's worth for all of the money we are spending, so that it should be possible to reduce the rate of health care cost inflation without harming patients. By that, I mean that we are systematically providing care that neither extends life nor improves quality of life, and in some cases we are reducing quality of life. If it were the case that all of our health spending was productive (improved quality of life and/or extended life), it would truly be difficult to identify reductions in planned expenditures that are necessary to make our system sustainable. That is not the case, which is good news, but that does not mean that it will be easy. If we systematically ask the three questions above, it will be exceedingly hard and we will make mistakes. If we don't try, health care costs will bankrupt our nation.

How Do We Start?

The process of transitioning to a sustainable health care system that is based on asking and answering the three questions posed above will take years to achieve, but all we can do is start from where we are. It has to begin with some steps, both big and small. We need more cultural discussion of these issues, but the best way to engender that is moving ahead on policy, because an overly abstract discussion will not be useful in helping us build a sustainable health care system with value at its core. The discussion has got to be practical.

The way to address cost inflation while keeping patient welfare in the forefront of the discussion is to focus on getting value for our money. Paradoxically, the increasing cost pressure in the health care system may be the only way to improve the value we receive for what we pay because worries about cost require us to pay closer attention to what we do throughout the system. The next chapter provides a set of concrete policy steps that I believe are the next (but not the last) steps toward developing a sustainable health care system.

Chapter 7
Health Reform: Next Steps

Health care costs are the biggest threat to our nation's long-term fiscal sustainability, and slowing health care cost inflation is a necessary, but not sufficient, condition of ever having a balanced budget again. The last chapter noted the cultural barriers to addressing health care costs, namely fear of death and our inability to discuss limits. However, we are who we are, and we must move ahead with a practical health reform strategy.

What our nation most needs is a bipartisan health reform strategy that will allow us to address the interconnected problems of the health care system: cost, coverage, and quality. There is no perfect health care system and no perfect plan. However, without a deal that allows both political parties to claim some credit as well as to have some responsibility in seeking to slow health care cost inflation, we have very little chance of success. Achieving a viable political deal for the way forward on health reform should be the top priority for anyone who claims to be interested in a balanced budget. Such a deal is not likely to yield tremendous deficit reduction in the short term (next 10 years), but fundamental reform is vital if we are going to have any chance of avoiding the unimaginable long-term deficits that will inevitably occur over the next three to four decades with our default health care system.

The ACA is the only viable reform vehicle that we have, due to three numbers: 218, 60, and 1. That is of course the number of members of the House, Senate and White House that must vote for any health reform change, be it a full-scale repeal or a small tweak (this of course could be changed by the Supreme Court). Significant reforms can be undertaken to the ACA to both improve it in terms of coverage, cost, and quality as well as broaden its political acceptability in ways that provide some credit to both Democrats and Republicans. Both parties will have to work together if we are to do the most consequential work of addressing and slowing the rate of health care cost inflation.

Overview of Suggested Reforms

The six concrete steps I propose as modifications of the ACA framework:

Replace the individual mandate with federally guaranteed, universal catastrophic insurance coverage

End the tax preference of employer paid health insurance

End the Medicaid program by transitioning responsibility of dual eligible Medicaid costs to Medicare, while moving non elderly low income persons into subsidized private health insurance

Expand the ability of Medicare to become an active health care purchaser and encourage in Medicare a culture of experimentation

Enact comprehensive medical malpractice reform

Adopt an overall cap on federal health care spending of GDP growth plus 1 percentage point starting in 2022, and back this up with a tax-based fail-safe

The following policies represent my understanding of what a compromise between the political parties would roughly look like if they negotiated a way forward and they were serious about addressing health care cost inflation, and taking account of the realities of the health care system and our current political and economic situation.

Replace the Individual Mandate with Catastrophic Coverage

Covering all persons with at least catastrophic insurance coverage is the correct thing to do in moral terms, and will provide a predictable source of health insurance coverage which I believe is necessary for achieving cost control for both technical and political reasons. It is wrong for our nation to spend so much on health care and not provide at least basic coverage for all citizens. We even require hospitals to treat all comers in emergency situations; it is time to take the steps to provide universal catastrophic coverage.

I would gladly trade federally guaranteed universal, catastrophic coverage for attaining 95% coverage with more comprehensive benefits via implementation of the ACA unchanged. This would allow Progressives and Conservatives to get what they most want in terms of health insurance: universal coverage and catastrophic, instead of first dollar coverage, respectively. If you hate one side of this deal, that is actually the point. To move ahead will take compromise.

Such a deal would make the individual mandate unneeded. It is unclear what the Supreme Court may rule about the mandate in June 2012. If it is upheld, a political deal is still needed to move ahead, and if the mandate is overturned but the rest of the law remains intact, consequential changes will be needed to achieve risk pooling. This compromise would allow President Obama and the Democratic party to take credit for compromising on their initial health reform law, and Republicans could take credit for getting rid of the individual mandate. Progressives will have achieved their long-term goal of universal coverage (that the ACA as is will not achieve), while Republicans will be bailed out from having to offer a comprehensive reform plan that can address costs and quality while expanding insurance coverage rates, which they do not have. It is telling that they made no progress toward a vision of what they were for since taking control of the House of Representatives. Without such a plan, Republicans have no hope of ever achieving a balanced budget.

The best way to implement catastrophic coverage is via Medicare (perhaps Medicare Part E) because it is simple, and could be implemented quickly. Conservative economist Martin Feldstein has suggested a federally guaranteed catastrophic insurance approach implemented via a newly created federal executive branch mechanism. Under Dr. Feldstein's proposal, individuals would get a voucher to purchase a private catastrophic policy and be issued a "federal health care credit card" to use to pay for care in the deductible amount if they wished, the size of which he reasonably suggests should be linked to income (he suggests 15% of adjusted gross income). The federal credit card he suggests would guarantee that providers would get paid, and would also provide patients with a guaranteed means of financing care, though they would be responsible to pay it back.

I prefer using Medicare as the catastrophic insurance vehicle, but might accept a mechanism like Dr. Feldstein's in lieu of using Medicare if it truly achieved universal coverage, though it is surprising to me that Conservatives would want to create a *new* federal apparatus to implement a catastrophic insurance plan. It is unclear whether the catastrophic policies available under Dr. Feldstein's proposal would differ by what was covered, or would they cover any care above the deductible amount? Finally, for a catastrophic proposal to work, providers will have to make public their prices ahead of time, or they could be linked to Medicare payments for simplicity. These are key issues that would have to be resolved under any catastrophic proposal.

Under my proposal, we would implement state-based health insurance exchanges in which insurance policies would be available for gap insurance. To reduce adverse selection, annual enrollment periods with guaranteed issue could be maintained. Certain care like well child visits and prenatal care could be made first dollar covered under a catastrophic policy. I suggest very large deductibles in order to maintain an important role for private health insurance in the system via selling gap insurance ($10,000 individual; $15,000 family, which would be indexed to medical inflation).

Either the amount of the deducible or subsidy provided with which to purchase gap insurance should vary by income. The same actuarial outcome could be reached by either approach, but I favor varying the premium support amount to be used towards purchasing gap insurance in order to maintain an important role for private health insurance. Deductibles and/or premium support could also be varied by age, say in 10-year bands, which would more closely link premiums to the expected cost of an individual's own care, and would lessen the degree to which young adults cross-subsidize those who are older in such a system.

Some persons would choose to stick with the catastrophic level of insurance, while others would want more coverage. People should buy gap insurance with after tax dollars. Employers could arrange and pay for gap insurance for their employees, but the premiums they paid on behalf of workers should be taxable income. I would expect employer involvement in insurance to decrease over time, which I think would be good on balance, so long as there is guaranteed catastrophic coverage and readily available insurance for gap amounts available through exchanges. This would end insurance-related "job lock" which may be a barrier to entrepreneurship. The reduction in employer role should lead to an increase in both tax receipts and disposable income, all else equal, as currently non taxable compensation in the form of insurance premiums shifts to taxable wages. States would have broad discretion in setting up insurance exchanges. There would be many details to work out, but if the parties could agree on federally guaranteed catastrophic coverage with a robust role for private insurance, the details should be tractable.

Cost Reduction

Providing universal catastrophic coverage may provide some downward pressure on health care costs, but likely not as much as some might assume. That is because of the distribution of high use and the cost of health care. If my family had a $15,000 deductible last year and choose not to buy a gap policy, in retrospect, we would have essentially been uninsured.

All five members of my family had an annual physical, one of us had a follow-up visit to investigate a chronic condition, there are four recurring prescriptions in our household, and there were five "sick" visits between the three kids, three of which resulted in one-time prescriptions. In addition, one of my children suffered a fairly significant sports-related orthopedic injury that resulted in an ER visit and a wrist being placed in a cast, and two follow-up orthopedic visits. All told, I estimate that we would have had around $7,500 in out of pocket costs last year had we paid it all out of pocket which we would have had to do if we had a policy with a $15,000 deductible and no gap policy. Of course, one of us could have had a very large health expenditure that ran into the hundreds of thousands of dollars; you only know you didn't suffer a profoundly catastrophic cost during a year until it is over.

For example, while in the ER with the orthopedic injury for one of my children, there was a point at which surgery for the broken bones appeared to be imminent because the doctors could not set the broken wrist. If surgery had been required, we would have blown through even a $15,000 annual deductible most likely in that day alone. And if the bones could not have been set, surgically repairing the wrist would not have been discretionary given the nature of the injury. A large deductible will exert some downward cost pressure on those with relatively low health expenditures, but will do virtually nothing for someone with extremely high ones. Especially after the annual deductible or capped annual out of pocket amount is reached, true catastrophic insurance that pays 100% of medical bills provides no downward cost pressure. High deductibles do the least to control costs for the patients with the highest costs, whose care drives our cost problem.

By comparison, during last year my family paid $4,000 in premiums and around $1,000 in out of pocket costs under our current insurance policy that is provided by Duke University (and Duke paid around $7,000 in premiums).

My goal in having a large deductible is to maintain an important role for private health insurance that would cover the "gap" which provides maximum flexibility for future reform efforts. I anticipate that most people would desire to purchase such coverage, but this approach would provide them with the option of only having truly catastrophic coverage that would protect the rest of us from massive medical bills that they could not afford if they were uninsured and got sick or injured.

Settle Coverage Questions and Focus on Costs

Settling the coverage issue would allow the singular focus of health policy to be addressing health care costs while seeking to obtain value for what we spend. And there are some subtle reasons that universal coverage is actually a precursor to increased efforts to address health care costs.

First, when providers, be they hospitals or physicians negotiate payment rates with insurers, the burden of providing uncompensated care is often specifically invoked as a reason for needing higher payment levels for care. I suspect this actually has a stronger impact on holding back cost control efforts than the actual magnitude of any cost shift to public and private insurers has, but that is only my intuition. Caring for the uninsured is a reality for providers (especially hospitals), but serves as a bargaining point used by hospitals for why lower payment rates proposed by public and private insurers are untenable. Universal catastrophic coverage would remove both real economic cost shifting as well as the hindrance that such care provides to focusing on cost reduction strategies.

Second, some form of universal coverage is needed politically if we are going to do the hard work of truly dealing with health care costs. We are currently in policy "no man's land" whereby we have various legal requirements and cultural expectations that mean the uninsured get some care, but not the fortitude to follow through with these notions and provide a system of universal coverage. That doesn't mean everyone has to have the same insurance or to choose the same options, but we need to take one variable off of the table, the issue of persons being uninsured, so that we can focus on costs and quality.

Reform the Tax Preference of Employer Paid Health Insurance

This is easily the most consequential policy that we could undertake to slow cost inflation in the private market within the current system. If we were going to do one thing and then see what happened before taking further steps, this would be it (if we couldn't agree to catastrophic coverage suggested above, for example). The Fiscal

Commission suggested this beginning in 2014 when the ACA exchanges will be up and running, and it has long been a mainstay of Republican health care plans, like the one offered by Senator McCain during the Presidential campaign, and the Patients' Choice Act, sponsored by leading Republicans in the 111th Congress.

The Medicare program is ground zero for the federal budget's unsustainability because it joins the demographic reality of the baby boomers with our nation's overall health care cost inflation problem. However, a cost reduction strategy that only focuses on Medicare will not work for several reasons. First, around half of total health system spending is in the private portion of the system. We spend more privately per capita than many nations spend in total. Second, the health care delivery system provides care to both Medicare beneficiaries and the privately insured. This is one of the reasons that Medicare is so popular among beneficiaries: it assures them access to mainstream health care services. Third, cost control in one portion of the system only may lead to cost shifting to other providers, namely private insurance. Some recent work on cost shifting by my co-blogger Austin Frakt who has resurrected a 20 year old book written by Michael Morrissey has suggested that cost shifting has a smaller impact than often assumed, with a larger Medicaid to private cost shift as compared to Medicare to private. However, there is an impact.

The bottom line is that that entire health care system has a cost problem, and cost control efforts must focus on all parts of the system. Changing the current tax preference provided to employer based insurance is the most obvious place to start to address costs in the private portion of the system.

Democrats have already voted for a de facto capping of this tax expenditure via the tax on high cost insurance, but the imposition of the tax was delayed until 2018 in the Reconciliation bill that completed the ACA. Moving to directly cap the tax exclusion earlier and making it apply to more policies would increase the cost saving potential of the ACA. If done in concert with moving to a guaranteed universal catastrophic insurance scheme this is really a conversion of a now-regressive tax expenditure (benefits high income persons more) to a more equitable distribution of federal support for catastrophic coverage. It would be transitioned into a progressive subsidy under what I suggested by providing income based premium support for gap insurance coverage. The goal should be to transition to the point whereby persons buy health insurance with after tax dollars and income-based direct subsidies, regardless of the exact next steps in health reform.

Move to End the Medicaid Program Over the Next Decade

I suggest we move to end the Medicaid program and begin to transition the following three groups of Medicaid beneficiaries as follows:

Acute care Medicaid would be covered by federally-guaranteed catastrophic coverage I suggest with states being responsible for premium support to purchase private gap insurance policies for them. There are 45–50 million such persons, and the ACA will increase this group by 16 million by 2021. These beneficiaries are numerous, but are the cheapest Medicaid beneficiaries on a per capita basis because most of them are young and relatively well.

The total cost of the *Dual eligible* beneficiaries will become the responsibility of Medicare, which now covers their acute care costs, while Medicaid currently pays for most of their long term care. There are around nine million such persons, and these are the most expensive persons to care for in the entire health care system on a per capita basis.

Long-term disabled who are not eligible for Medicare will be covered by federally-guaranteed catastrophic coverage supplemented by state-paid gap insurance. There are around five million such persons. This is a varied group with many different types of needs, and will likely be the most complicated group to transition away from Medicaid.

Ending Medicaid would represent a profound change in the insurance system of our nation and will likely be controversial for both Progressives and Conservatives. Progressives will worry about transitioning acute care Medicaid into the private insurance market and how vulnerable persons will fare; Conservatives will worry about placing the entire long-term care responsibility for dual eligible seniors with the federal government. This direction is justified by a mix of policy and political reasons.

In policy terms, the division of responsibility for care of the dual eligibles causes outcomes that are suboptimal in both quality and cost terms. The proposed changes are warranted purely on policy grounds for the dual eligibles.

Other proposed Medicaid changes are motivated more directly by political concerns. Conservatives seem to viscerally dislike Medicaid because it is a government insurance program, while Progressives believe its safety net function is vital to the well-being of our country. I believe the political viability of Medicaid as currently structured is in doubt, and that budget pressures will cause incremental reforms that will chip away at the safety net provided by the program. In the current climate, Medicaid is being looked to shoulder spending cuts in an unthoughtful manner. Progressives need to drive changes to the program in order to protect vulnerable beneficiaries, and there are incentives for both Progressives and Conservatives to transition away from the current program.

The logic behind the proposed changes rests in the different needs of the "three programs" represented within Medicaid. Those covered by *acute care Medicaid* (45–50 million persons), most of them pregnant women and children, are relatively inexpensive to care for on a per capita basis. Increasingly, such beneficiaries have trouble finding providers who will care for them, due to a double whammy of stigma (it is insurance for persons who are poor) and the fact that it pays providers below what Medicare pays, which is less than what private insurers pay. This has led to a systematic access problem for some Medicaid beneficiaries who have trouble finding a physician willing to treat them. There is nothing inherently wrong with the structure of Medicaid; we could decide to make it the best payer of care tomorrow, but that of course is not going to happen. Buying them into private insurance policies will mainstream their care and remove a layer of cost shifting.

The second portion of the Medicaid program, the *dual eligibles* (nine million persons) are Medicare beneficiaries due to their age, or because they are permanently disabled, and covered by Medicaid because they are poor. Medicare should become responsible for all of their care, and states should no longer have any responsibility. These individuals are among the sickest and costliest persons in the health care system. Many such persons live in nursing homes, and some became impoverished due to paying for nursing home care, while others were poor prior to their entry into a nursing home.

The reasons to federalize all costs of the *dual eligibles* are both to improve quality as well as to incentivize one payer to reduce costs. There are numerous care coordination problems related to caring for dual eligibles that both increase the cost of their care and likely reduce the quality and appropriateness of what they receive that could best be addressed by making Medicare responsible for financing all of their care.

I will give two examples.

The first is bed-hold payments by state Medicaid programs, which are payments made by Medicaid to a nursing home while a dual eligible beneficiary is in the hospital, which is paid for by Medicare. The motivation for such payments is sound—maintaining a place for such a person to return when an acute hospitalization ends. However, the incentive created is for nursing homes to send patients to the hospital when they are very ill, and have high acuity. This is medically appropriate if there is a hospitalization that can address the problem being faced by the person that cannot be addressed in a nursing home. However, such admissions often provide little value to patients and in many cases may harm them, even as they drive up overall costs.

A related example is that *dual eligibles* living in a nursing home may be prevented from electing the Medicare hospice benefit due to the interaction of their state's Medicaid nursing home rules and Medicare hospice regulations (Medicaid hospice policies differ by state). Around nine in ten Medicare beneficiaries who receive hospice do so in their homes. For many dual eligibles, the nursing home is their home. However, in some states, electing the Medicare hospice benefits affects the person's Medicaid status, causing them to have to pay for the room and board portion of the nursing home bill (most of it) while they receive Medicare-financed hospice benefits. The impact of this policy is shown by the fact that Medicaid decedents who die in a nursing home have a lower probability of using hospice prior to death than do others, even though the care hospice offers would be relevant to most of them.

For the sickest, most vulnerable members of society, having one insurer responsible for all of their care is the best way to improve the quality and appropriateness of their care, and perhaps to reduce the overall cost by reducing the incentives for one government payer to shift costs to the other.

The third portion of the Medicaid program are the *long-term disabled* (five million persons) who are not eligible for Medicare, which means they are younger than age 65. This group would include those with mental and intellectual disabilities and those with long-term physical disability due to a catastrophic event such as a stroke or spinal cord injury. The most reasonable strategy would be for states to retain the responsibility for acute care gap insurance (they will be covered by federally guaranteed catastrophic coverage) purchased in exchanges. The federal government could provide a subsidy to states for the additional care and services needed for this relatively small, but very vulnerable patient group. I am open to suggestions on how this group can best be provided with the services they will need for years, and in some cases, decades.

The use of Medicaid as a coverage expansion vehicle in the ACA was understandable, but I believe that the long-term political future of Medicaid is in doubt and that Progressives should lead the drive to transition away from it as a program. Moving to end the Medicaid program in a manner that ensures that the needs of beneficiaries is provided for would remove an entire layer of cost shifting, and end a program that is tainted by the stigma of being associated as a poor people's insurance. Proposals to block grant Medicaid do not account for the distinct nature of the three "programs" within Medicaid, and it is best to move proactively to modernize and improve the Medicaid program than it is to let it die by a thousand cuts. Under a "slow death" scenario for the Medicaid program, dual eligible and long-term disabled beneficiaries would be those most at risk due to their high needs and the per capita cost of their care.

Expand Medicare's Ability to Be an Active Purchaser

Medicare has long been a passive payer, and essentially covers all non experimental services that are agreed to between provider and patient. We need to take a variety of steps to empower the Medicare program to exert more purchasing authority over what it pays for, and in doing so begin to incorporate an expectation of patients receiving value for all that Medicare purchases. These three questions need to become front and center in all that Medicare does:

> Does it improve quality of life?
> Does it extend lifespan?
> How much does it cost?

Only by pulling together such information and using it to inform Medicare payment and coverage decisions can we truly begin to reduce health care expenditures over that level that would be expected under the status quo. Consequential policies to address such questions head on would have direct effects on Medicare and might be expected to have spillover effects into private insurance. Such changes in Medicare are needed regardless of whether we adopt a universal catastrophic coverage approach or not, and are likely even more important if we simply move ahead with implementing exchanges absent a shift toward universal catastrophic coverage that I have suggested. In short, regardless of the exact structure of any system moving forward, private health insurers will likely find it politically difficult to limit their coverage of nonproductive care if Medicare continues to cover such care.

A few concrete ideas.

Expand the Authority of the Independent Payment Advisory Board

The idea of Independent Payment Advisory Board (IPAB) is to empower a board of experts that is granted authority to make Medicare policy in a manner that is insulated from Congress. As passed in the ACA, it can only propose changes in payment rates under limited circumstances. I would greatly expand the IPAB to allow it to systematically look at both coverage and payment rates and methods. After watching the debt-ceiling "debate," it seems noncontroversial to me that Congress is incapable of making the very difficult decisions that will be required to address health care costs in a reasoned manner, and that a model of experts making detailed assessments with Congress maintaining an ability to vote up or down on their recommendations is the best way to make Medicare a more active purchaser of health care.

For example, IPAB could focus on common and expensive diseases for the Medicare population, such as congestive heart failure (CHF) and apply the definition of value that I provided earlier: does it improve quality of life? Does it extend life? How much does it cost? Answers to these three questions are needed, along with broad discussion to decide if a particular treatment is "worth it."

Results from such a review could produce different layers of changes. For example, treatments that are shown to be nonproductive could be deemed to be ones that are not generally paid for by Medicare under certain circumstances. Others which are marginally productive could be paid for with a higher out of pocket cost share, or could be subject to reference pricing meaning the payment of a lesser amount that is equal to a more proven therapy that is less expensive. Providers would have to accept the lesser reimbursement for the procedure or treatment. There should be no limitation placed on what individuals can spend their own money on, but this would be setting explicit limits on what public money would cover in certain circumstances. The details of working this out are obviously important, but the default is that we never get to the details because we constantly avoid the difficult decisions in health care.

IPAB focuses on Medicare, but could have an impact on cost in the overall health care system. Recall the story from Chap. 6 about Blue Cross Blue Shield of NC being unable to carry through on their plans to limit access to a type of surgery. At least part of the story was that Medicare pays for the surgery with virtually no questions asked, so then how could a private insurance company move to limit access to the procedure? Reducing health care costs will require either less care be provided and/or providers be paid less for care on a per capita basis as compared to the default case. We must develop an ability for someone to be able to say no, or we will not address health care costs.

Give the Kitchen Sink Approach to Improving Quality and Reducing Costs a Chance to Work

The ACA has numerous pilot projects that are designed to test new models of health care that could move us away from our current fee for service-driven system and toward one with different incentives (away for incentivizing illness and intense medical treatment). The key to best using the various tests of models and approaches in the ACA is to depoliticize them. Some things will work, some will fail. That is why we are trying new approaches. We need to move these inevitable tinkerings into the realm of policy and out (somewhat) of the realm of politics. Examples include the Office of Dual Eligibles, pilot projects on new approaches to delivering concurrent palliative and hospice care (delivery of such care without a patient having to unelect curative treatments), the development of new models of care delivery like Accountable Care Organizations (ACO) and the like.

The biggest hindrance to being able to learn from any of these demonstrations at this point is the politicization of health reform. Both parties need a way to take some credit for health reform, and most importantly to have some responsibility for taking the next steps to address costs. This would enable us to best use new information.

Experimentation with Competitive Bidding

Competitive bidding aims to bring market forces to bear on health care costs and quality through insurance companies competing for business. The big idea of the ACA is to provide governmental subsidy to enable the purchase of health insurance that varies by income with patients choosing among options to harness competition. At the big picture level, there seems to be some similarity between the exchanges in the ACA and the proposal by Rep. Paul Ryan to transition Medicare to a private insurance system in which beneficiaries purchase their own coverage using a government-provided voucher. The idea of competitive bidding was given added political credence in December 2011 when Rep. Ryan and Senator Ron Wyden (D-OR) endorsed a competitive bidding approach for Medicare that would maintain traditional (fee for service) Medicare as an option. This was a departure from Rep. Ryan's earlier proposal that was passed in a budget instruction by the House of Representatives in April 2011 which would eventually end traditional Medicare, but that proposal had no chance of enactment, and was not even taken up by the committees in the House of Representatives that would have had to complete the details.

In policy terms, competitive bidding is an old idea, but in the political realm, the joining of a Democratic and Republican elected official to support a consequential health reform is big news.

There are two problems in getting to the bottom of the similarities and the differences of a variety of health reform plans that use the phrase competitive bidding and/or premium support: language and the details.

I distinguish three approaches to purchasing private health insurance with support from the government to defray the cost. They may seem similar, but are very different in reality. And within each of these three varieties noted below, there are innumerable policy distinctions that could be made. Within the broad category of premium support, the version below that I term competitive bidding is an idea worth trying, in both the elderly and nonelderly population. The other two are probably not.

The first approach is the use of an *Equal Value Voucher*. An equal value voucher is when everyone gets the same amount of money to go and purchase health insurance. The main effect of such an approach is to fix the total cost to the federal government, and essentially to shift cost differences to individuals. This is not being actively proposed by anyone as a Medicare policy, but this is similar conceptually to block granting the Medicaid program to the states. The federal government would fix their cost and shift the remainder to the states in the case of Medicaid, or to the patient if you had an equal value voucher proposal.

The second approach is an *Administratively Set Voucher*. This is where an amount is provided to people that enables them to purchase private health insurance, but the key detail—how much money is provided to purchase insurance—is set administratively as opposed to by market forces. The current Medicare Advantage program, and really all earlier variants of Medicare HMOs were administratively set vouchers. The amount of money provided was determined in relation to the average adjusted per capita cost (AAPCC) of Medicare in a given county; it was set at 95% of AAPCC for two decades in an attempt to reduce costs until the mid-2000s, when the amounts were greatly increased with a policy goal of increasing participation in private plans. However, the amounts were still administratively determined. A company that could provide care cheaper than the value of the voucher simply pockets the difference as profit.

Rep. Paul Ryan's plan passed by the House in April 2011 to transition over time away from the current Medicare program and toward a system of providing money for the elderly to purchase private health insurance is also an administratively set voucher program. In fact, his linking of the amount provided to the elderly in the future to purchase health insurance to overall inflation, which grows much less slowly than health care inflation, shows what can happen with an administratively set voucher program: the value and therefore purchasing power of the voucher would greatly erode over time.

Competitive bidding occurs when the amount of a voucher provided to a patient with which to purchase private health insurance is determined by the actual cost of an insurance policy that covered a set of services (defined benefits) in a given health care market. This price would differ by market, and would be set through competitive bidding, in which insurance companies were each seeking as much business as possible. Setting the voucher amount at the price at which the lowest bid company was covering the specified benefit package would incentivize other insurance companies to aim to provide better care for less money and therefore gain market share. Insurers could compete on provider network, wellness programs, or internal efficiency. If insurers charged a higher premium than this competitive bid standard for a given area, the patient would have to be willing to pay the extra amount if they wanted to sign up for the higher priced plan, as the government would only pay the lowest bid amount in a given market. If properly constructed, cost could drop and quality could increase.

The ACA exchanges are the closest thing we have to competitive bidding at this point, although there are worries that the premium subsidies provided in the out years could erode under some circumstances. Competitive bidding is a good thing to try in the exchanges, and it also a reasonable thing to try in Medicare. The key is that the amount of premium subsidy provided to patients must be set by the cost of an actual reference health insurance policy that is readily available in a given market.

Senator Wyden and Rep. Ryan's plan proposed in December 2011 may fall in the competitive bidding realm, because of how the amount provided by government to Medicare beneficiaries would not be set administratively, but would be set via a bidding process between private insurance companies (note: the details are important and the plan is not in legislative language as of this writing). Further, this proposal would maintain traditional Medicare, though it would have to live under the limits of the competitive bidding framework as well, with patients receiving cash payments if plans (or traditional Medicare) were able to provide health care to their covered population for less than the competitively determined bid amount, and being expected to pay more if the premium was higher.

Competitive bidding should be the standard in the exchanges as well as for any private options in the Medicare program. Both "sides" of the current political debate are hypocritical. If competitive bidding is good and acceptable for the ACA exchanges, then why would it not be acceptable as an option in Medicare, and vice versa? Competitive bidding could probably be implemented in some fashion even if we adopted a guaranteed catastrophic insurance plan that I suggest. An insurance company could receive the same premium necessary to purchase the federally guaranteed catastrophic coverage, and this option of choosing a private insurance company for all care could be made available.

In policy terms, something like Wyden–Ryan will likely be adopted one day in Medicare, for both political and policy reasons. I used to call for an end to private insurance options in Medicare. However, having no private insurance option in Medicare is a fantasy of the left, just as having no public option (traditional Medicare) is a fantasy of the right. Given that there will likely be some sort of private insurance option in Medicare along with a public one, I think that some version of premium support based on competitive bidding could be better than our current Medicare Advantage program. And we must do something. The Wyden/Ryan plan continues that part of the conversation.

It is true that Rep. Ryan moved to the center from his initial Medicare proposal, but that only means he moved away from his fantasy with respect to Medicare, as have I. However, I am unable to give a final grade to the Wyden/Ryan proposal without knowing what we will do to expand coverage (or not) for people under the age of 65, while seeking to slow costs and improve quality. If Wyden/Ryan were a part of a deal that also adopted a compromise to modify and implement the ACA, then this is potentially a way forward (but more details are needed). Rep. Ryan continues to maintain an inconsistent rhetorical stance since the introduction of Wyden–Ryan in December, 2011: arguing that exchanges are a key aspect of Medicare reform, while also being terrible for the US health care system for persons who are younger than age 65.

Medical Malpractice Reform

Medical malpractice reform is a perennial campaign issue for Conservatives, often sold as a panacea for fixing the cost problems of our health care system. This is a common view among physicians as well. Last year I spoke in an annual meeting of a medical specialist society, and there were innumerable physicians convinced that capping noneconomic damages in lawsuits would reduce health care spending by one-fifth overnight (a recent op-ed on the subject making this claim was floating about). I kept asking the physicians asserting this if that meant their income would drop by one fifth overnight given that payments to physicians are the second largest category of medical expenditures in the nation? They looked at me like I had three heads in a way that said "that is not what we had in mind!" I bet.

In reality, medical malpractice is a far better campaign issue than it is a policy that could revolutionize health care costs. However, Progressives should take this campaign issue away from Conservatives by enacting malpractice reform, both because there are big problems with this aspect of our system as well to render the issue politically moot.

A malpractice lawsuit claims that a doctor treated a patient negligently, that this treatment caused harm, and it seeks monetary compensation. Negligence means that a physician failed to provide the standard of care expected by the prevailing medical custom. Juries decide cases that are tried, but most cases are settled or dropped. Lawyers get paid (typically 35%) only when they win or settle a case.

A successful malpractice system would protect patients from harm via a deterrent effect of lawsuits, compensate patients for harm and exact justice. In addition, a good system would protect physicians from frivolous suits, identify substandard physicians so that medical licensure boards could remediate them or remove their licenses and provide a clear signal to insurers regarding the risk of insuring a physician.

Our malpractice system does none of these well.

Some basic facts: About four in ten lawsuits are filed when there is no physician error. Such cases usually do not result in awards but are stressful to physicians. However, only two in 100 cases of truly negligent care result in malpractice claims being filed, leaving the vast majority of the worst care unaddressed. And when negligent care is identified via a suit, the compensation for harm is inefficient, with 55 cents being spent administering the system for each dollar paid to injured patients.

The result is physicians who feel under assault from the malpractice lottery, patients who remain at risk of substandard care, and injured persons who may not receive enough compensation.

Malpractice increases costs primarily through defensive medicine—the ordering of unnecessary tests, consultations and procedures designed to demonstrate care and caution to use as a defense if a physician issued. Defensive medicine is estimated to increase system costs by 1–9%. At 5%, this would amount to $125 billion per year. I suspect that actual savings from even the most robust malpractice reform would be far less, primarily because there are multiple motivations for what is termed defensive medicine, including habit, monetary incentive and a culture that assumes more is better.

Even though addressing it is no cost-saving panacea, malpractice reform that is responsive to physician concerns is a crucial stepping stone to the type of comprehensive reforms that are needed to achieve a sustainable health care system. We must slow the rate of growth in health care costs, and it will take big changes throughout the system. We will not achieve this without the buy-in of doctors, whose professional judgment runs the health care system.

My experience with physicians who are colleagues and friends suggests that, though physicians differ in many ways, they have one similarity: an obsession with getting sued. I think this is borne of the cost (time and money) of their training and the fear that one lawsuit could take it all away. I have heard many physicians say that, although income is important to them, what they really would like is to practice medicine as a calling and not to constantly worry about getting sued and paying high malpractice premiums. We should take them up on this offer.

First, we should adopt a series of reforms discussed during the ACA debate and scored by the CBO as providing around $54 billion in deficit reduction over 10 years that provides for a federal cap on noneconomic damages in lawsuits among other things (the AMA endorses a $250,000 cap). In return, all persons need to be insured with at least catastrophic coverage, reducing the pressure of having to sue to obtain money needed to finance care for a person rendered uninsurable due to an injury.

Second, we need to transition from addressing medical errors via an oppositional system toward one focused on patient safety and learning from mistakes. This openness is impossible in the current system. As part of this change, the medical profession would have to take more seriously the policing of its own.

Third, we should reconsider how liability insurance is provided. Many factors related to rising malpractice premiums have nothing to do with claims experience, including investment losses of insurance companies, insurance losses in other sectors and marketing behavior in which insurers cut premiums to gain market share only to raise them rapidly later to avoid insolvency. We need stable insurance that reduces physician worry, is consistent with a patient safety approach, and compensates injury efficiently.

Finally, and perhaps most importantly, we need physicians to lead the way in systematically reconsidering how medicine is practiced in the United States. We cannot afford the current system, and we are not getting our money's worth from what we spend. Currently, any large change in the system would be met by most physicians with the retort: What about lawsuits?

No nation has succeeded in major reform without supportive physicians. The only way to get from here to there is to give physicians a substantial victory in the area of malpractice and then to appeal to their professionalism and sense of calling to care for patients in helping us create a sustainable health care system.

Cap Federal Health Spending Backstopped by a Tax-Based Fail Safe

The Fiscal Commission adopted a series of health policy recommendations most notably suggesting a budget cap on combined federal health care spending: Medicare, Medicaid, the Children's Health Insurance Program, Federal Employees Health Benefits (FEHB), TRICARE (which covers families of active duty military personnel), the ACA exchange subsidies, and the cost of the tax exclusion for health care. They propose that beginning in 2020, this total federal expenditure and subsidy of health care be limited to grow not faster than 1 percentage point faster than the entire economy (GDP plus 1 percentage point). If such a rate of cost inflation in all federal health spending were not achieved after 2020, then Congress would be required to enact additional policies to slow cost growth in the overall federal contribution to health care.

I believe this is a good policy to apply a cap to total federal health spending, whatever the eventual makeup of those categories may be (I have suggested ending Medicaid, for example). However, I suggest adding a second-step trigger should these cost growth targets not be met—an increase in the payroll tax, implemented on wage earners above the median wage and applying to all wages earned if this target (no greater than GDP growth plus 1 percentage point) is not met *and* further attempts to slow the rate of health care cost growth fail. The tax would be paid only by the employee, and not the employer. The amount of such a tax would be determined by the magnitude of the cost overrun, but for placeholder purposes, I would suggest a tax of 0.5% of payroll, applied to the top half of the wage distribution.

The point of such a tax is to put in place a clear choice for the public. We can set target growth rates for total health care spending, and say that we want to address health care costs but we seem to hate any policy with a chance to actually slow such costs. By setting the growth rate in total federal health care spending at 1 percentage point above the GDP growth rate, we are saying our federal spending on health care will grow faster than everything else in our economy, but that there are limits. If we don't reach our growth goal, then Congress and the President can put in place policies that will constrain the growth of federal spending. However, if history is a predictor of the future, there will be a backlash and it will be hard to constrain health care cost growth. In that case, we will simply have to pay more in taxes to support cost inflation above the growth target. Such a tax, implemented only after policies to constrain growth are tried (or not), will provide us with a very clear choice: continued inability to slow health care cost growth will have to be paid for via higher taxes. The goal of my suggested policy is to make the choice clear and real.

I Do Not Favor Raising the Medicare Age

I do not suggest raising the Medicare age as a policy option, because it mostly shifts, and doesn't reduce costs. Removing the youngest and therefore healthiest sliver of the Medicare program will not revolutionize the cost of the program, but would shift some costs from the federal budget onto beneficiaries or to another aspect of the federal government (income-based premium support, for example). In fact, recent analysis suggests that doing this will increase overall health care spending, because all such a policy does is to move persons out of the largest risk pool (Medicare) into a smaller one.

As a stand-alone policy, there is no doubt that raising the Medicare eligibility age is a bad one. And doing so assumes the implementation of exchanges under the ACA. However, I am open to raising the Medicare age in a manner that equalizes it with the Social Security retirement age as part of a broader political deal that either brings about federally guaranteed universal catastrophic coverage or an agreement to move ahead with implementation of the ACA that makes reform the responsibility of both parties. For many Conservatives, a move such as this one is a strong signal of seriousness in addressing long range health care cost problems. As I say, I don't think they are correct, but there is a policy logic of increasing the age along with Social Security increases given that they have been linked for so long. In the end, I would potentially agree to this, so long as what is gained in return is consequential enough.

If we did raise the Medicare eligibility age, it would work as follows. Increase the Medicare eligibility age by 2 months/year beginning in 2014 until it reaches age 67 in 2025. A person who turns 65 on January 1, 2014 would be eligible for Medicare on March 1, 2014. A person turning 65 on January 1, 2015 would be eligible on May 1, 2015 and so on. This will not revolutionize the cost structure of the Medicare program, and in fact will remove the actuarially cheapest patients from the program (the youngest). 2014 is key, because that is when the exchanges will be up and running.

The Social Security retirement age is already set to increase in this manner as set by the Social Security changes adopted in 1983. Historically, the age for Medicare eligibility and full retirement (you can retire currently at age 62 and receive a lower Social Security benefit) have been the same and this change would continue that practice. Doing so would reduce Medicare outlays by around $100 billion over 10 years according to the CBO, but would have a far larger reduction in federal spending in later years once the eligibility age was 67 while it is now projected to be 65. However, if this change is made in isolation, it simply shifts costs and doesn't reduce them.

The Way Forward

We need a series of changes to the ACA that allow it to stop being the symbol of political toxicity, and transform it into a bipartisan vehicle to address the health care cost problem that is at the heart of our nation's long-term fiscal woes. Slowing the rate of health care cost inflation relative to the rest of the economy compared to historical trends is a necessary, but not sufficient condition to ever achieving a balanced budget. We need to act soon, and the ACA is the only viable reform vehicle that we have. Reaching such a compromise along the lines that I suggest would allow both parties to receive some credit, and most importantly, would mean that both parties share responsibility for seeking to address health care costs while addressing the related problems of coverage and quality. This must occur for us to have any chance to ever have a balanced budget again.

Chapter 8
Social Security

Social Security is first and foremost a retirement income program that provides other, less well-known protections, such as income support for children if a parent dies, and disability insurance. Fifty-six million people receive benefits from Social Security, with 69% of them being retired workers and their families, 12% being survivors of deceased workers, while 19% are disabled persons or their children.

The program is the cornerstone of the safety net in the United States, and perhaps most importantly defines the income below which we will let no elderly person fall. Prior to the advent of the program in the 1930s, more than half of the nation's elderly lived in poverty, while today fewer than one in ten do. Around 15% of all elderly persons have no source of income other than Social Security, and one in four depend upon it for 90% of their income. Therefore, a predictably functioning and sustainable Social Security system is among the top Progressive priorities.

Many Progressives view any discussion of reforms to the program with fear and trepidation. It seems as though we think that discussing the need for reform or comparing the various options somehow places the program at risk. This is especially true because the program can pay the scheduled benefits for another 25 years with no changes. So why entertain a discussion of policy options that, once begun, could lead to program changes that are not to the liking of Progressives?

It is a fair question. I believe that there are several benefits to moving sooner rather than later to reform Social Security.

- The program must be eventually be reformed because the taxes to be collected do not match the promised benefits over the next 75 years. The shortfall is equal around 0.7% of GDP over this time period. In 25 years, this shortfall will cause a precipitous drop in benefits of 20–25% absent action. Moving now to reform the system provides more time for changes to take hold, allowing Progressives to argue for changes that strengthen the program in line with Progressive priorities.
- There is no guarantee that Progressives will be in a better political situation at some later point when Social Security reform may be completed.

Because Social Security provides cash to beneficiaries that are indexed in some way or another to inflation, it is a very predictable program. Cost savings from health care reform (whether via the Affordable Care Act or any alternative that may be developed) will be far more speculative and unpredictable, simply because it is more complicated to purchase health care than it is to mail checks. If we arrive at a bipartisan Social Security reform agreement, then it can be expected to work roughly as planned, truly taking Social Security "off the table" and allowing us to focus on health care costs.

Finally, moving with a serious reform of the program may also provide opportunities to argue more broadly for general tax increases that will be necessary if we are to achieve a long-range balanced budget. In one sense, if Progressives move now to reform Social Security, they will call the bluff of Republicans who believe that we are afraid to move first in reforming our sacred cow. By doing so, Progressives will expose Republican unwillingness to consider theirs: the raising of taxes that will inevitably be a part of any long-range plan that produces a balanced budget.

Principles for Social Security Reform

There are several key principles for Social Security reform. First, all changes need to be clear and understandable to all generations. Second, we should increase the minimum retirement benefit, or the floor below which no elderly person shall be allowed to fall. Third, we must increase the tax revenue flowing into the program. Fourth, we should reduce benefits for higher wage retirees. Fifth, we should reduce benefits for all beneficiaries by linking their growth over time to general inflation and not wages. Via a mixture of benefit reductions and tax increases, we can make the Social Security program able to pay the newly identified promised benefits over the long run without raising the full retirement age.

The Nature of the Problem

The problem facing Social Security is purely demographic. The movement of the baby boom generation into eligibility for the program means there will not be enough workers paying payroll taxes at current tax rates to allow for the benefits promised in current benefit schedules to be paid. This is not a new problem, but has been inevitable since the mid-1970s when it was clear that the birth rates of the late 1940s to the mid-1960s indeed represented a "boom." There is simply a financial shortfall between the taxes that fund Social Security and the schedule of benefits that are due to be paid over the next 75 years.

While life expectancy has risen since the advent of Social Security in 1935, that is not the primary reason that there is a long-range Social Security financing problem.

The Nature of the Problem

The biggest problem is no more complicated than the baby boomers had fewer children than did their parents. Social Security (like Medicare) is a pay as you go program which means that current workers pay payroll taxes to finance the retirement costs of current retirees. Paying into the system gives one a right to later collect benefits, but this is a social contract, not an annuity contract. In 2000, there were around four persons paying payroll taxes for each Social Security beneficiary; in 2030, there will only be 2.4.

The current unfunded Social Security liability—or the amount by which current promised benefits are larger than current anticipated taxes—is around 0.7% of GDP over the next 75 years. By comparison, the unfunded liability of the current Medicare program absent changes for the next 75 years is on the order of 4–5% of GDP, a much larger problem. To provide further context, the current Social Security payroll tax is 12.4% of all wages up to $106,800. If the payroll tax were raised immediately to 13.98% of payroll up to $106,800, and this rate remained constant and the wage to which the tax is applied is updated as scheduled for the next 75 years, the shortfall would be completely made up.

In public policy, it is always good to keep in mind the default option. What happens if we do nothing? In the case of Social Security, it means an across the board benefit cut on the order of 20–25% in around 25 years. The reason is that starting in 2010, less money in payroll taxes flowed into Social Security than was paid out in benefits. This meant that Social Security had to begin redeeming special treasury bonds that were purchased by the federal government with excess (more than benefits to be paid out) Social Security payroll taxes in the past. When more money flowed into Social Security than needed for benefits, the surplus was used to underwrite the federal government's debt. Essentially, the right hand loaned the left hand money, to be paid back later. For the next quarter of a century, Social Security will receive this money back in order to pay benefits. This process will continue until there are no longer any treasury bonds earmarked to Social Security remaining, which should happen in about 2037 according to the latest CBO estimates.

Under current law, once this occurs benefits paid out must equal the payroll taxes that flow in during a given year, which will require the large benefit cut noted. Should this take place, in the worst year (year with biggest shortfall sometime in the mid-2040s), payroll tax revenues will be able to cover about 75–80% of the currently promised Social Security benefits, according to the CBO. This is the default way that Social Security's financing problem will be dealt with: a substantial cut in benefits in about 25 years and continuing thereafter.

This is where the politics come in, and where both Conservatives and Progressives have it wrong on Social Security.

One the one hand, Conservatives typically overstate the magnitude of the problems facing the program. Many political speeches given by Conservatives on the federal budget often make some sort of joke or assertion whose punch line is that workers in their 20s and 30s who are today paying payroll taxes will receive *nothing* from Social Security. This is an absurd overstatement that is not based in fact. In fact, if we did nothing to Social Security, then benefits would be cut to around 75% of their current level in about 25 years; not my preferred choice, but a far cry from nothing.

Progressives often assert that Social Security reform is not a top priority because it faces a smaller problem than does Medicare, or because the program can pay the scheduled benefits for the next quarter of a century. While both of these statements are true, they miss the negatives of waiting and the positives of moving sooner to reform the program. If we wait for a debt-driven crisis in the future to address the program shortfalls, there will be fewer options and austere cuts will be more likely to occur. Likewise, beginning inevitable reforms sooner provides more options and allows for changes to be gradual, and leave the opportunity for improving Social Security in such as increasing the minimum benefit. Progressives often seem think that discussion of Social Security reform is a danger to the program and seem to think that delaying discussion of reforms that are inevitable is protecting the system. In fact, delaying action to address the problems of Social Security likely puts the program at greater risk because of the uncertainty of the makeup of any future Congress and White House that will someday have to take up the issue, perhaps in the midst of a debt-driven crisis with little leeway.

What About Life Expectancy Gains?

A great deal of the rhetoric arguing for the need for Social Security reform invokes increases in life expectancy since the program was initiated in 1935. The logic goes that since the life expectancy of the population has increased since the program began, shouldn't the age of eligibility for benefits also increase? Of course the full retirement age will begin to rise slowly in 2014 (2 months/year) until it is 67 in 2025. However, many argue for a further increase in the retirement age for full benefits.

In response, it has been pointed out that life expectancy gains have not been uniform across the population, and that gains for lower income persons have been much more modest than have the gains for higher income persons. This is a factually non-controversial assertion; the top 50% of the income distribution has experienced a far larger increase in expected age at death than have those workers in the bottom half of the income distribution. This means that an increase in the age of expected full retirement benefits under Social Security will disproportionately harm lower income workers because they will have a shorter period of time collecting benefits than will higher wage workers. However, that is true today when the Social Security retirement age is 65 and would be true even if the Social Security full retirement age were decreased due to the fact that persons with lower income die younger, on average.

It is a classic example of how many of the political and policy debates are not discussions at all, but simply amount to different groups repeating their preferred fact over and over and saying it supports their preferred policy option. It is undoubtedly true that life expectancy has risen since Social Security was introduced many years ago. It is also undoubtedly true that lower income workers have not seen their life expectancy increase by as much as higher income workers.

The financing problem facing Social Security is not primarily driven by life expectancy changes one way or another, but instead by the decline in the number of workers paying payroll taxes per beneficiary. So, which ever fact about life expectancy that you find most compelling (it has increased; not as fast for the poor, etc.), it doesn't really provide a complete answer for how to shore up Social Security over the long run.

Specific Social Security Reforms

There are two ways to extend the ability of Social Security to pay out its promised benefits: either increase the taxes flowing in or reduce the promised benefit levels; of course a mixture of these two strategies could be used. There are a variety of detailed plans that would extend the solvency of the Social Security program, typically employing a variety of policy changes that include the raising of some taxes and the curtailing of some benefits. Below I provide an outline of my preferred solution for fixing Social Security and taking it off the table; the cost estimates given are based on a CBO analysis of different options to reform Social Security.

The overall calculus needed to fix Social Security is a mixture of increased taxes and reduced benefits minus any expansion of benefits to add up to around a 0.7% of GDP over the next 75 years. Some of the policies I suggest actually increase the cost of Social Security over this period, which simply means that offsetting increases in revenues or decreases in certain benefits must be identified to bring the program into balance.

Expand the Safety Net by Enhancing Low Income Earner's Benefits on the Basis of Years Worked

The benefits provided by Social Security are modest, and many elders rely solely or nearly so on Social Security payments. This is why the across the board benefit cut that would occur in 2037 in the absence of any reform would be so devastating. By reforming Social Security now, we can expand the minimum benefit for low income workers by giving them increased credit for years worked. This essentially raises the benefits that such workers will receive. CBO estimates that this would cost around 0.3% of GDP over the next 75 years. That means I have added to the problem right off the bat, and must do even more in the way of increased taxes and/or reductions in other benefits.

Increase the Amount to Which the Social Security Payroll Tax Is Applied

To make up the shortfall (which is on the order of 1.0% of GDP over the next 75 years after increasing the minimum benefit), I would suggest raising the wage cap to which the OASDI payroll tax applies.

This tax increase is reenacting the essence of the 1983 Greenspan Commission policy that extended the actuarial balance of the of the Social Security program until 2037: apply the Social Security payroll tax (OASDI) to all wages of nine in ten Americans (the 90th percentile of wages). In 2010, the OASDI payroll tax is applied to the first $106,800 of wages, which is approximately the 83rd percentile of US wages. So what happened between 1983 and today?

During the past quarter century, salaries of the highest wage earners have risen much faster than average earnings, but the rate of increase in average earnings has been used to update the wage limit that is subjected to the OASDI payroll tax. In 2012, the scheduled maximum to which the OASDI payroll tax will be applied is $113,700; the 90th percentile of wages will be around $156,000 in 2012. This of course is an increase in taxes. I believe that it is worth it to ensure full payment of Social Security benefits for elderly persons with no other source of retirement income. And it is further worth it to me to ensure that persons with private sources of retirement have a predictable amount of retirement income that is not dependent upon the state of the stock market at the time they retire. Finally, the increase in taxes will expand the benefits of higher income workers because the Social Security benefit formula provides for higher returns given higher payment of payroll taxes.

This would add around 0.2% of GDP to the equation, so puts me needing to identify around 0.8% of GDP in increased taxes and/or reduced benefits to achieve balance.

Reduce Initial Benefits for Higher Income Persons

To do this I would lower the initial benefit formula for the top half of the earnings distribution, which would add around 0.4% of GDP to Social Security. This would amount to a benefit cut for persons in the top half of the income distribution. This leaves me with 0.4% of GDP that still needs to be made up.

Change How Benefits Are Calculated and Updated for All Beneficiaries

There are a variety of policy options to change how benefits are updated or indexed over time. Doing so amounts to a cut in benefits as compared to the currently promised benefits and I propose doing this to partly bring the Social Security program into long-range actuarial balance. The two options I propose are changing the way benefits are currently calculated and replacing that with a two-part formula to determine initial benefits (which will provide 0.2% of GDP). The second option is to change how benefits are updated, or indexed by linking this to overall inflation instead of to wages (the so-called chained CPI-U), which also results in a benefit reduction that will yield 0.2% of GDP. These benefit reductions would be offset for lower wage earners by the increase in minimum benefit noted above. This mixture of benefit reductions and tax increases would put the Social Security system on a strong footing for the next 75 years.

Do Not Raise the Full Retirement Age

I would prefer to achieve actuarial balance for the Social Security program without raising the full retirement age above the slow increase already planned that will make the retirement age 67 in 2025. CBO has estimated that raising the full retirement age to 68 would make up around 0.1% of GDP and raising it to 70 would provide around 0.3% of GDP in improvements to the Social Security actuarial balance, each over the 75 year time horizon. Many Conservatives favor raising the full retirement age and I wouldn't rule that out in light of the fact that we need a bipartisan way forward, but it is really a matter of what they are willing to give in order to take this step. I would prefer raising the Medicare eligibility age (assuming a readily available source of health insurance for persons) to raising the Social Security age, though doing that is not my preferred option either. A raising of the full retirement age along with a separate retirement age for persons working in manual labor jobs could be undertaken and is conceptually pleasing, but it seems difficult to implement this simply.

Another reform that is worth considering is a tweak to Social Security that would build in protection against the elderly outliving their private retirement assets. Jed Graham, a reporter for Investor's Business Daily, has written a book outlining "old age risk sharing" which is interesting and worth considering, and the Fiscal Commission noted reforms that could have a similar effect. Such a policy would lessen benefit levels at younger retirement ages, and in return, benefit levels would rise with age instead of being flat. In this way, persons living to very old ages would receive accelerating benefits as they aged. This type of reform could be undertaken at no net cost to Social Security, but that would raise issues about lower benefits at younger ages and how this will impact low wage and manual workers who will be less likely to survive into the accelerated benefit period.

Payroll Tax Cut

The OASDI (Social Security) payroll tax was cut from 6.2% of wages up to $106,800 to 4.2% for 2011 as part of the deal to extend the income tax rates that were set to rise to pre-2001 levels on January 1, 2011. Republicans and Democrats joined to keep the payroll tax at the current level (4.2%) through 2012. There are several issues that deserve comment about this policy.

First, the holdup to extending the payroll tax cut for the entirety of 2012 was how to pay for it or offset the decreased revenue to the federal treasury by budget cuts.

It was not paid for, which makes sense if the payroll tax cut is designed to be a stimulative countercyclical policy (increased governmental spending during economic down turns). Given that interest rates are at historically low levels, this made sense.

Second, the payroll tax cut does not undermine the future of Social Security; the payroll tax reduction is simply an efficient means of increasing the take home pay of persons with wages that are subject to Social Security payroll taxes. Money is borrowed by the federal government equal to the revenue that would otherwise be lost, so does not worsen the finances of Social Security.

Third, once the payroll tax has been decreased for two straight years, it is unclear politically how it is easily restored, especially as an isolated policy. The logic of reducing the payroll tax was to provide a short-term stimulative effect. However, the politics of the payroll tax cut then are fraught with danger for Progressives, who have given leverage to Conservatives to argue for changes to the Social Security program generally, in return for an increase in the payroll tax to earlier levels. In one sense this simply ups the stakes for a potential lame duck session of Congress in which not only will the income tax code be set to increase, but payroll taxes as well.

The Way Forward

The Social Security program is a key Progressive priority that can actually pay out full scheduled benefits for 25 years. I have not made detailed proposal to fix the system, but have instead provided a general outline, relying on general options that have been laid out by the CBO. For me, the bigger priority is moving sooner rather than later to shore up Social Security for the long run, which will allow for changes to the program that actually improve its protection of the poorest seniors. And because the program is simple, if an agreement is reached it will work as expected and could truly be "off the table," allowing us to focus on the issue of health care reform and addressing health costs which will take years of tinkering and experimentation to get straight, with many inevitable tweaks and changes. Agreeing to a reform that aligns the promised benefits and taxes of Social Security over the long run will also demonstrate that we can solve problems, which would be good in terms of both providing reassurance to financial markets as well as providing some hope to all of us that our political system can address our problems. For all these reasons I believe that Progressives should be willing to move ahead on Social Security reform now.

Chapter 9
Guns vs. Medicare

Guns versus butter is the classic example of a public finance tradeoff given in a high school economics text to signify the hard choices that society must make. Guns, of course, signify investing finite public resources in military spending, while butter signifies doing so in goods and services such as health care, social services, and infrastructure. The goal of policy is to obtain the correct mix.

That we should have a federal military budget should be uncontroversial since Article I Section 8 of the US Constitution explicitly names spending for "Common Defence" to be a federal role. However, the size of our military, both with respect to the spending levels of other nations as well as with respect to the other parts of the federal budget, is open for debate.

Total military spending is around $680 billion this year, with around $180 billion of this going for the ongoing cost of the Wars in Afghanistan and Iraq. The War in Afghanistan is now the longest ever fought by the United States, and we have had soldiers in that nation longer than did the Soviet Union. The past decade has seen large supplemental military expenditures of around $1 trillion (that were not included in the overall federal budget), to fight these wars. Normal military spending accounts for roughly one-fifth of the federal budget. If we are going to develop a sustainable federal budget, all spending categories, including the Military budget must be reduced over current baselines. As the fighting in Iraq and Afghanistan is winding down, some savings will be realized. However, further reductions are needed if we are to achieve a sustainable federal budget.

I am not a military or foreign policy expert, but I am a citizen who is interested. My observation is that discussion of US military spending is some of the least thoughtful budget discourse. Some deem military spending to be "off limits" and it seems as though no amount could possibly be enough for them. Other reflexively state that the military budget is worthy of massive cuts, with little or no thought given to how these cuts should be implemented and at what cost to the security of our nation and our allies.

Military Spending in Context

I think of military spending in conjunction with health care spending. Even though there may seem to be no obvious connection between federal military and health care spending, they are linked in two ways. First, they are very large line items in the federal budget. Taking the current budget, the military consumes about 20%, while Medicare alone consumes 14% (and Medicaid 7%). Fast forward 10 years, and current projections show that military and Medicare will each account for two in ten dollars of the federal budget. Second, when comparing budget categories cross-nationally, the two areas in which we most stand out are spending on the military and health care. We not only lead the way in per capita spending in these two items, but we do so by a long shot.

If you believe that military spending should not be cut at all, or only very little, then you really must be serious about reducing health care costs. If, on the other hand, you are willing to enact substantial cuts in the military budget, this lessens the degree to which we will need to slow the rate of health care cost increases. In this way, the guns vs. butter debate is really guns vs. health care. Or more specifically, guns vs. Medicare.

Cross-National Military Spending

There are two ways to characterize military spending: as a percent of our economy (GDP), and in direct comparison with the amount spent by other nations. One shows the relative share of our economy devoted to military spending, and the other provides a means of directly comparing our spending to our potential enemies.

Even as military spending has surged with two wars the past decade, we spend less on our military in percent of GDP terms (4–5%) than we did during the buildups of the 1980s (7%), and far less than we did during World War II (about one-third) or Korea (around 15%).

The most important way to describe military spending is in actual dollars compared to the rest of the world, and most importantly, the nations we are most likely to fight in a war. In 2009, our defense budget constituted 46% of the *entire world's* military spending. In other words, nearly every other dollar spent on defense in the entire world was spent by the US government. And many of the nations that spend quite a lot on military outlays are our allies.

The combined military budgets of Cuba, Iran, Libya, North Korea, Sudan, Syria, China, and Russia totaled about $170 billion in 2009, or one-fourth of what the United States spent on the military in that year. As a citizen it strikes me that we need to think about military spending in terms of multiples of what our most likely enemies spend. And then we need to ensure our military is configured to fight the types of wars that we are most likely to face. Our current spending seems excessive, and a reasoned discussion of the size and mix of military spending in needed.

Fiscal Commission Recommendations

The Fiscal Commission report proposed $200 billion in defense cuts between 2012 and 2022. Their logic was that there needed to be a separation between defense discretionary spending and nondefense, and that both parts of the discretionary budget (not Medicare, Medicaid, Social Security) should share equally in the needed cuts over the next decade or so. These recommendations seem plausible, especially from the perspective of domestic discretionary and military expenditures being available for budget reductions. Further, the Fiscal Commission did have the assistance of military experts of both political parties available to them in developing their recommendations, and 12 currently serving members of Congress served on the commission whose recommendations enjoyed some bipartisan support.

The recently passed Budget Control Act of 2011, the deal to raise the debt ceiling, enacted "security" cuts of $380 billion over 10 years (this includes the Department of Defense, Homeland Security, Foreign Aid, and Veterans Affairs). This appears to be a larger cut to defense than suggested by the Fiscal Commission, but it is more complicated to determine that since it refers to more than just the department of defense. It is worth noting that President Obama's 2012 budget requested cuts to the department of defense of $400 billion over 10 years.

Chapter 10
How Much Should Government Spend?

In the abstract, everyone wants lower taxes. And while many people say they want lower government spending, the preferences they give about specific programs do not seem to back up this assertion. If the public holds inconsistent views about their preferred level of taxation and spending, how can we ever develop a sustainable budget? Are the problems an irrational public? Or the way in which the questions and choices are framed?

An interesting study from The Program on Public Consultation at the University of Maryland School of Public Policy was released in Spring 2011 that provides some insight into this conundrum. The authors frame their study against a backdrop of polls that seem to provide irrational responses to the budget deficit, which they feel occurs because of how information is provided in polls.

> The purpose of this study was to give a representative sample of Americans the chance to deal with the problem of the budget in such an integrated framework, one in which they would make tradeoffs. The goal was to have respondents face the kinds of challenges that policymakers face when making a budget. In this way we can see whether Americans are able to deal with such a challenge, and whether they in fact know what their value priorities are.

Part of the problem is the difficulty in grasping the relative magnitude of the dollars at stake in different parts of the federal budget. Numbers that are enormous (millions) in our common experience are insignificant in the context of the federal budget (billions, trillions). For example, the Republican leaders in the House of Representatives have noisily debuted a program during the 112th Congress called *You Cut*, in which citizens are asked to pick amongst a series of programs to be cut each week. For example, the week of July 4, 2011, they had three programs on the chopping block:

Refocus National Park Service Spending, save $157 million
Terminate federally funded junkets for University Professors, save $15.3 million
Terminate a pilot program that pays Food Stamp recipients to consume more fruits and vegetables, save $20 million

Leaving aside the relative merit of these spending programs, and the language they use to frame them (junkets instead of trips), a *You Cut* program that was designed to be consequential in achieving a sustainable federal budget would look more like:

End the Home Mortgage Deduction, $100 billion
Cut the Defense Budget by 10% annually, $50 billion
Cap the tax exclusion of employer paid health insurance at the median premium, $50 billion

It is simultaneously true that $15.3 million is a lot of money while also being a trivial amount in the context of the overall federal budget. The Republican *You Cut* initiative is designed to give supporters who are opposed to government spending in the abstract, a feeling that Republicans in Congress are addressing the fiscal problems facing our nation, while simultaneously deflecting attention from the true sources of our fiscal unsustainability.

Can the Public Decide?

The University of Maryland study mentioned earlier was designed to address misunderstandings and framing errors by working with the staff of the President's Fiscal Commission to design study materials that would allow citizens to make informed tradeoffs. The first step was splitting the budget into Medicare and Social Security since they have dedicated funding streams, as distinct from the discretionary budget (incl. defense). They did not address Medicaid in the study given its complex (federal/state with relative cost share amount differing by state) funding arrangements. Participants were given detailed choices that provided both the dollar value as well as the magnitude of the fiscal shortfall in that budget silo that would be rectified by a given choice.

The 1,250 participants reached a surprising level of consensus about how to reduce the deficit that results from the discretionary spending portion of the budget.

The average choices of all groups reduced, but did not eliminate, the default discretionary budget deficit of $625 billion that is projected for 2015, via a mix of spending cuts and tax increases. Independents and Democrats achieved the most deficit reduction while those self-identifying as tea party sympathetic had the highest remaining deficit in 2015. All four groups identified substantial spending cuts and tax increases that lessened the deficit due to the discretionary portion of the budget by one half to three quarters.

From the initial $625 billion projected discretionary budget deficit in 2015, the average choices of the groups left the following deficits in 2015:

Independents $124 billion
Democrats $130 billion
Republicans $294 billion
Tea Party $337 billion

When it came to Medicare's contribution to the deficit (projected at $400 billion in 2015), the participants had a harder time. Four options were highlighted:

Increasing payroll taxes
Increasing Part B premiums
Raising the Medicare eligibility age
Reducing payments to physicians

A majority viewed none of these options as being acceptable. The most popular proposal was a one percentage point increase in the Medicare payroll tax that was viewed as acceptable by 33% of respondents and tolerable by nearly another half. Interestingly, this most popular measure would generate around $68 billion in revenue in that year, or three times *less* revenue than the average amount of revenue increase embraced by the most tax-averse group when focusing on the discretionary budget.

This is an important finding because it suggests that respondents had more trouble identifying ways to trim the Medicare-generated deficit as compared with the discretionary budget deficit, including defense; this is consistent with what I wrote earlier about our cultural views of health care and how they impede reform.

Respondents were not eager to raise taxes or premiums or to reduce benefits by increasing the eligibility age when focusing on Medicare. Neither were they eager to reduce Medicare payments to doctors. However, Medicare is a key driver of the long-term deficit, and it is not possible to obtain a balanced budget via cutting discretionary spending only. More importantly, Medicare's contribution to the deficit is accelerating over time.

When it came to addressing the portion of the deficit produced by Social Security, the respondents were a bit more successful than with Medicare and embraced a mix of tax increases and reductions in benefits for high wage earners and increasing the eligibility age for Social Security gradually. Interestingly, a majority of respondents in this exercise favored increasing the minimum benefit that Social Security provides (increasing the safety net feature of the program) even though this meant that more tax increases and/or benefit reductions for higher earning beneficiaries were then needed. This implies that study participants were taking a highly nuanced view and while committed to addressing the budget shortfall of the nation, were doing so with a strong sense of priorities and a willingness to invest even more resources in certain areas because they represent strong priorities for them.

The Public Finds Health Care Choices Harder

On the whole, this exercise shows that with good information, members of the public can make hard choices, though they do not do equally well across parts of the federal budget. The public seems more able to engage in tradeoffs in the discretionary area of the budget (including military) and Social Security, but seems to have more trouble in the area of Medicare.

What does this mean? What can we do to counter the seeming unwillingness of the public (even when educated and provided information in a meaningful manner) to identify ways to slow Medicare costs even as many say we must do so? It is not entirely clear, but the earlier chapters focused on health policy in this book make a strong case for the "specialness" with which many persons view health care. That is why health reform is so politically charged, because so many people feel very vulnerable and worried about health and health care. This is bad news because health care is at the heart of the unsustainability of the federal budget.

The difficulty of the decisions that need to be made on health care often drives the deficit discussion to very noisy disagreements about irrelevant items of federal spending. In our highly politicized nation, we seem unable to have a conversation for fear of losing out to the "other side" and much of the debate about the budget deficit focuses on relatively small sources of domestic spending that are not the main source of the problem in any event.

We tend to move almost seamlessly between two perspectives with respect to small programs. We defend those we like in part by saying they are inconsequential to the overall problem, while condemning small programs favored by our political opponents. For example, I have (rightly in my view) derided the *You Cut* program and mocked the size of the three programs put forth in the first week of July 2011 for cuts. However, in the same week President Obama castigated the Republican negotiators in the debt limit talks for refusing to change the manner in which corporate jets are amortized. For Progressives, this is a sign of an out of touch Republican party (how can they defend such tax breaks for the rich at a time like this!), while Republicans note derisively that changing this aspect of the tax code will barely dent the long-range budget shortfall of the United States. And people who buy corporate jets hire people, including the folks who make the jets!

The tables are exactly turned when discussing the proposed *You Cut* programs, with Republicans saying how can we afford those faculty junkets, while Democrats may say but that spending is trivial in the grand scheme of things. And on and on with noisy and unproductive disagreements that help us to ignore the truly hard decisions required to address the drivers of our long-term deficit.

Setting a Target for Balance

We need to set a target at which to achieve a balanced budget, and to then engage the program by program decisions that would be required to achieve balance at a given level of GDP. This will give us the best chance of having a reasoned, rational discussion that can be informed by the tradeoffs of spending and taxes that will be necessary to achieve a balanced budget. Only with a firm guidepost of a percent of GDP at which to seek balance can we do this.

For the past 40 years, taxes have averaged around 18% of the GDP, and spending has averaged a bit less than 21% of the GDP. This means that we have typically had a budget deficit of around 3% of GDP since I have been alive. The problem is that the movement of the baby boomers into eligibility for Medicare and Social Security will upset this calculus, and much larger deficits will occur by default, simply due to paying for normal functions of government.

The Fiscal commission set the target balance point at 21% of GDP—an increase in taxes received over the typical amount collected in the past 40 years, and a spending cut over the very high current spending levels, pushed to 25% of GDP by a smaller GDP and emergency spending. It is worth noting that 20.6% of GDP is the largest amount of tax revenue collected in the past 40 years (in 2000), so 21% would represent a level of taxation not seen before. Of course, this is why we have typically had a budget deficit since spending has commonly been higher than 21%—in 1970, 1975, 1980, and 1985—for example. It is also worth noting that when we commonly spent more than 21% of GDP in the 1970s and 1980s the baby boomers were largely working and paying payroll taxes. Having spending at 21% of GDP as the baby boomers transition en masse into eligibility for Medicare and Social Security will require fairly aggressive cuts to planned spending in these programs. It is plausible that we can do it, but it will not be easy.

The Committee for a Responsible Federal Budget (CRFB) has prepared a useful table that documents 32 deficit/debt reduction plans that have been put forth by a series of think tanks, prominent economists, and individual politicians. It is a sign of the shifting public discourse that groups left, right, and center have seen fit to publish more or less detailed plans on how they would achieve a stabilization of the cumulative debt and movement toward a balanced budget.

The President's Fiscal Commission proposed capping revenue at 21% of GDP and aims to balance that with spending of 21% of GDP by the year 2035. By 2020, their approach would have spending at 22% of GDP and revenue at 20.5%, with debt held by the public stabilized at 65% of GDP.

The Heritage Foundation and Americans for Tax Reform have put forth the most austere proposal that would cap revenue at 18% of GDP, and they claim this could be achieved by 2020 (spending and revenue at 18% of GDP). Other groups and liberal politicians have not proposed clearly delineated revenue caps, which I view as target points for balancing the budget, but there are a variety of more liberal plans that would seek balance at around 22–24% of GDP. The most credible liberal plan is the Center for American Progress plan which would achieve balance at a bit over 23% of GDP in 2035.

I believe that 21% of GDP as the target for capping tax receipts and seeking balance at this level over the next 20–25 years is a reasonable target for several reasons. First, the Fiscal Commission was populated by some of the key politicians who will have to agree to some sort of consensus way forward if we are to ever attain a balanced budget. Republican Tom Coburn of Oklahoma, and Democrat Dick Durbin of Illinois, who sit quite far apart on any measure of Conservative/Liberal ideology, both voted in favor and said they did so because any plan that could lead to a balanced budget would include things that Conservatives and Liberals dislike. Interestingly, five of the six Senators on the Fiscal Commission voted yes, while five of six House members voted no.

Second, the Fiscal Commission plan has now been widely vetted through various policy and political circles. Because the plan meticulously identified a vast array of policy decisions that would trim spending over current levels and increase taxes, it provides a "marginal analysis" against which other ideas can be raised. There exists a sense among many that the last step toward developing a long-range plan for a balanced budget will be similar to what the Fiscal Commission came up with, but the hard part is figuring out what the first steps to get to that point are.

There remain the true believers on both sides who say that 21% of GDP collected in taxes is way too high or way too low, but by laying out a clear target of 21%, perhaps the most important thing that the Commission report did was identifying a measuring stick for different approaches.

For example, Rep. Paul Ryan's budget proposal aims to cap spending at 19% of GDP, a lower level than that suggested by the Fiscal Commission. One of the ways in which Ryan would achieve balance at a lower level of spending is by transitioning Medicare to a voucher program in which beneficiaries would purchase private health insurance for persons who are 55 and younger today. This would reduce federal expenditures earmarked for Medicare substantially, but would provide elders with less generous coverage, and shift the cost difference to the elderly. It is a bold proposal and it is legitimate to try and argue the case, but it would appear that Rep. Ryan has already failed in this effort since neither the House Republican-led Ways and Means committee nor Commerce committees have even held a hearing, much less a full committee mark up of these ideas for reform of Medicare. The proposal proved too politically unpopular.

Without a health reform plan that can drastically reduce health care spending on Medicare, there is no hope of a balanced budget, certainly not at 19% of GDP. Therefore, there is no reason to believe that this proposal will succeed because it would require profound changes to Medicare that at this point he cannot even get discussed in the key health policy committees in the House of Representatives.

On the other hand, the plan from the Center for American Progress is much more plausible as a plan to balance the budget simply because they are willing to raise taxes high enough to generate 23% of GDP by 2035. I think this level of balance is too high and is not likely to emerge from the sort of political consensus we need, but it is important to state that it is a credible means of producing a balanced budget.

Much public education and discussion will be needed if we are to achieve a balanced budget. Without a target percent of GDP at which we are aiming for balance, it is impossible to have a meaningful discussion about what changes to spending and taxes will be required to achieve balance.

Chapter 11
Tax Reform

There are two main reasons to levy a tax. The first is to try and reduce the occurrence of an activity or a type of behavior. Excise taxes on cigarettes are an example. The second reason for a tax is to raise money to fund spending priorities at levels that markets would not provide.

In the early 1930s, the market had spoken in terms of retirement income. More than half of the elderly persons in the nation lived in poverty in the aftermath of the Great Depression. Likewise, in the 1960s the market had spoken in terms of health insurance for elderly persons, as around half of them were uninsured.

The creation of Social Security and Medicare were explicit statements that what the market was providing for Seniors in the way of retirement, and health care was socially unacceptable. So, taxes were levied and these programs were designed to provide retirement income and health insurance for older persons. And in doing so, income was redistributed. That is what government spending does; it redistributes income. People who would have lived below the poverty line did not, and a great deal of health care was financed for the elderly that they otherwise would not have received. Lifespan has increased and disability from many conditions has declined.

In the case of Social Security, payroll taxes are the means of financing the program (6.20% of payroll paid by employer and employee from the first dollar up to $106,800 in wages, currently). Medicare is financed by payroll taxes (Part A, hospital insurance is financed by 1.45% of wages paid by employer and employee, applied to all wages) while income taxes and individually paid premiums fund the Part B doctors insurance portion of the program.

Other federal spending is financed primarily by income taxes, both individual and corporate.

Mix of Federal Taxes Over Time

The mixture of taxes employed by the federal government to raise revenue has changed substantially over the last 75 years. The amount of federal tax revenue collected by excise taxes and corporate income taxes has declined, while revenue from personal income and payroll taxes has risen.

In 1935, when Social Security was passed into law, excise taxes on items as diverse as steel, tobacco, and alcohol accounted for four in ten dollars collected by the federal government; in 2010 they accounted for just two in 100 dollars of federal tax revenue. Income tax receipts represented 15% of total federal tax dollars in 1935, but from 1945 until current day have accounted for between 40 and 50% of all federal tax receipts, and remain the largest source of revenue for the federal government today. Payroll taxes for Social Security and Medicare have risen from 1% of total receipts immediately after the passage of Social Security in 1935, to 40% of federal receipts in 2010, 46 years after the passage of Medicare. The share of federal tax revenue collected by corporate income taxes has plummeted from 35% in 1945 to 7.2% in 2010, and has not been above 10% of total federal tax receipts for the past 30 decades.

Key Goals of Tax Code

If we are going to ever have a balanced budget at any level of spending that is remotely realistic, then tax receipts will have to rise over current levels. I have set 21% of GDP as the amount of federal tax revenue at which to seek a long-range balanced budget. All taxes change people's behavior in some way, so getting the optimal tax rate for economic growth while raising the revenue necessary to pay for the agreed upon level of spending is not simple.

Reform of the tax code means determining the best mix of taxes to raise the revenue needed to fund the spending we say we want. Personal income and payroll taxes account for around eight in ten dollars collected annually by the federal government, and I approach tax reform assuming this will remain the case. The following four principles guide my thinking on tax reform. First, the tax code must collect enough money to pay for the spending we want in the long run. Second, the tax code must be viewed as fair and legitimate by most people. Third, it should be straightforward and understandable so that the incentives inherent in whatever tax code is adopted are clear. Fourth, it should incentivize economic growth in our economy, and the creation of jobs.

The hardest of these four is actually the first: committing to have a tax code that raises enough money to cover the spending we say we want. This is a choice. If you want more spending, it will take more taxes. If you want lower taxes, we will have to cut spending. Most people essentially want low taxes and high spending, but that is how we have managed to have a long-term fiscal imbalance that must be addressed.

We have to develop a tax system that is viewed as fair, and that people can understand. During a recent conference I attended, a presenter said the following: "half of all Americans don't pay taxes." He meant that half of all Americans don't pay federal *income* taxes, which is true, and is a testament to the fact that personal income tax rates have fallen drastically in the past 30 years, and are among the lowest in the world. But, that is not what he said.

The phrase half of all Americans don't pay taxes is of course false: payroll taxes for Social Security and Medicare are applied to the first dollar of wages, and anyone who buys something pays a sales tax. However, the sentiment behind the statement and the nods of people in the audience signaled their gut that they are paying the way for others in a manner that is unfair.

This was a group of relatively high income professionals. After my presentation, several approached me to say their tax burden was unfair and we needed to reduce spending and cut taxes. I asked if they wanted to end tax code provisions like the tax deductibility of mortgage interest and receiving tax free income via employer paid insurance, tax expenditures that disproportionately help upper income citizens like themselves. Several told me that I was making this up—government spending only helps poor people! Others said that aspects of the tax code that benefit some taxpayers but not others weren't spending programs, or didn't provide them with a subsidy. Others acknowledged the existence of these large tax expenditures but said that they deserved them because they worked hard.

An important part of developing a fair tax system is for everyone to understand it, particularly, how tax expenditures work and serve to increase the budget deficit in the same manner that explicit government spending does. The simpler the tax code the better so far as the clarity of incentives concerned.

Finally, a robust and growing economy is key if we are going to have a balanced budget, so any changes in the current tax code need to incentivize economic growth and job creation. This is especially important given the current weak state of our economy.

Fiscal Commission Tax Reform

The Fiscal Commission provides a detailed plan for comprehensive tax reform and is a general approach that I support. Their goal is to develop a tax code that could generate 21% of GDP, the point at which balance is to be achieved by 2035 when spending should decline to that level. Because there has already been some political buy-in by members of both parties voting for the Fiscal Commission proposals, this makes their recommendations a good place to start. I will focus my comments on income taxes, both personal and corporate since I have addressed payroll taxes in the health care and Social Security chapters (7 and 8), and I propose no changes other than those already noted.

Income Tax Rates

The current federal income tax has six rate bands:

10%
15%
25%
28%
33%
35%

Our tax code is progressive, which simply means that higher marginal tax rates apply to income above certain threshold amounts. Someone with an income of $50,000 would pay more on his or her last $5,000 of income than they would for his or her first $5,000. For example, the first $8,500 of income for all taxpayers is subjected to a tax rate of 10%. Bill Gates pays 10% of his first $8,500 of taxable income just like a person with an income of $50,000 would pay 10% of his or her first $8,500 in income (note that aspects of the tax code such as the Earned Income Tax Credit mean that approximately half of all households owe no income tax). Income between $8,500 and $34,500 is subjected to a tax rate of 15% and so on. The top marginal tax bracket of 35% is applied to all income above $379,150.

The Fiscal Commission proposed replacing these six marginal tax brackets with just three brackets; the rates in the three brackets would depend upon other decisions that must be made about tax expenditures, or policies that provide subsidy to certain situations or types of activity, like the Earned Income Tax Credit, or the home mortgage deduction. The Commission proposal very usefully demonstrates the relationship between the number of tax brackets, the marginal tax rate in each bracket, and the number of tax expenditures maintained in the tax code. For example, if *all tax expenditures were ended*, then the three tax rates proposed by the Commission are:

8%
14%
23%

If only two tax expenditures that are designed to aid lower income persons and families were maintained (earned income tax credit and child tax credit), then the three rates would be:

9%
15%
24%

As you add tax expenditures, the tax rate must go up just as it would have to if you add direct spending, if your goal is to generate the same amount of revenue and maintain progress toward increasing tax receipts and achieving a balanced budget by 2035.

The Fiscal Commission put forth a list of tax expenditures that might be retained such as the tax deductibility of mortgage interest on a first home, the Earned Income Tax Credit, Child tax credit, deductions for charitable giving. If this were the policy, then the three marginal income tax rates would be:

12%
22%
28%

These are the three suggested rates under the assumption that while most tax expenditures could be expected to be ended or reduced, we would be unlikely to end all such provisions of the tax code.

Another key aspect of the Fiscal Commission report recommendation is to treat dividends and capital gains as normal income and do away with a separate rates and rules for such income received from business investments or the sale of stock. The recommendations of the Fiscal Commission are premised on the idea of lowering the marginal tax rate and broadening the base of income that is taxable by limiting deductions, credits and exclusions. They note a possible modification of this proposal, which would be to exempt the first 20% of capital gains or dividends in an effort to encourage business investment. If this policy were chosen, then they proposed offsetting the lost revenue by raising the top (28% above) marginal tax rate.

The recommendation of making capital gains and dividends taxable as normal income is a good one, in conjunction with a broadening of the tax base, simplifying the tax code and dropping the marginal tax rates.

End the Corporate Income Tax

The Fiscal Commission suggests lowering the corporate tax rate to 28% from 35% in conjunction with reduction of loopholes, deductions, and exemptions to provide incentive for business to invest in the United States and create jobs. However, I believe that Progressives should propose ending the corporate income tax in order to provide the maximum possible long-run incentive for companies to create jobs in the United States and to do business here. In *conjunction with ending the corporate income tax*, the following modifications would be needed:

Capital gains and dividends should be taxable as normal income
Increase the top marginal tax rate above the 28% noted above
Enact a federal estate tax of 45% on amounts above $3.5 million

While US personal income tax rates are quite low by international standards (only Japan and Ireland have lower personal income tax rates), the stated corporate tax rate is quite high by comparison. There is a worry that this provides a disincentive to doing business in the United States and causes large corporations to move business to other nations. However, the effective tax rate paid by corporations differs wildly and very few pay anywhere near the stated rate of 35% of income due to exemptions, deductions, loopholes, and exceptions granted to particular businesses or industries. Public utilities are the only group of corporations that consistently pay anywhere near 35% of their income.

At the other end of the spectrum, General Electric infamously paid no corporate income tax in 2010 even though it earned $14.2 billion in profits. Some say that this was due to income being reported in overseas holding companies, while General Electric says that it was due to losses in the financial sector; so the facts leading to their paying of no corporate taxes are in dispute, and my brief research into the matter doesn't make clear what interpretation is correct. That is actually the most important thing to know about General Electric's (lack of) tax liability—it is confusing, hard to understand, but obviously legal given how high profile their lack of paying corporate income tax has been.

Ending the corporate income tax is obviously not a typical Progressive policy suggestion, and many Progressives will likely be thinking the opposite is true: we must figure out a way to extract more tax revenue from corporations. There are several reasons why I believe that it is a good idea to move in the opposite direction.

First, there is no greater Progressive priority than encouraging job creation and growth. What our country most needs now are good jobs, and ending the corporate income tax should directly stimulate job creation by making available more funds for businesses to use for investments, and provide long-range certainty about the fact that the United States is a good place to do business. While the rhetoric around job creation typically centers on small businesses, large corporations are the source of most jobs. In theory, the end of the corporate income tax should spur a great deal of investment and job creation. If it did, that would be great news for the country and the general fiscal situation (increased income taxes, increased payroll taxes, less unemployment benefits, reduction in Medicaid eligibility). A hiring and job creation boom would be the most important Progressive policy outcome that could come to pass.

Second, corporate income taxes are a relatively small portion of the total federal tax revenue collected, just 7.2% of total federal receipts in 2010, and from 10 to 13% of total receipts over the past 15 years. The revenue would have to be replaced by other sources and I suggest a higher personal income tax rate in the top bracket, perhaps from 28 to 30%, with the full value of dividends and capital gains being taxable as normal income as noted.

Third, part of the reason that the proportion of federal receipts that flow from corporate taxes is so low is that most corporations pay an effective tax rate that is much lower than the stated marginal rate of 35%. The only corporations who seem to pay anything near the full rate are public utilities. Other industries such as those in high tech industries pay very little in corporate income taxes, and there was the General Electric case already noted. There is a sense in which corporations cannot effectively be taxed due to their ability to lobby, and to move income and business around the globe. Lobbying for changes (deductions, exemptions, credits) in the corporate tax code may have a spillover effect in making the personal income tax code less efficient. It is simpler and more realistic to simply end the corporate income tax than it is to fight this battle, especially given the potential for this change to incentivize job creation.

Fourth, the huge differential in effective corporate tax rates makes any sort of tax reform very difficult because many industries have a great deal to lose, and they presumably have gotten their current very low effective tax rate due to their political clout. If there is a reduction in loopholes and deductions for corporations and a lowering of the rate to 28% from 35% as the Fiscal Commission proposes, this will likely represent an effective corporate tax *increase* for some (many?) industries. They can be expected to fight this vigorously. So, the only type of corporate tax reform that may be politically plausible is the ending of the tax altogether.

Finally, from a political standpoint, ending the corporate income tax would remove a powerful rhetorical device from Conservatives about the role of the tax code and job creation. A common narrative for Conservatives is that the reason the economy is not producing jobs is that taxes on businesses are too high. If the corporate income tax is put to zero, then it can hardly be claimed to be too high. I believe that there is likely to be both a real as well as a qualitative effect to *eliminating* the corporate income tax. Politically, this will rid Conservatives of an incessant arguing point that taxes are too high and that Progressives do not support business. If corporate tax rates are simply lowered, even to 1%, then Conservatives and the corporations themselves will still say they are still too high.

It is true that many corporations have a great deal of cash on hand currently, and that has not led to massive job creation, but instead a tepid job growth even as corporations have made a great deal of money. This is worrying, but ending the corporate income tax and increasing the highest rate of the personal income tax seem to be both a more predictable source of raising federal revenue as well as providing the maximum long-range incentive for corporations to do business in our nation and produce jobs.

Another key point is that a reduction of the corporate income tax rate to 0% would have to be done in concert with a comprehensive reform of the personal income tax code to be a viable option. Particularly important would be clarification of what constitutes a corporation? The logic of ending the corporate income tax only makes sense if dividends and capital gains are taxed as normal income, and further that loopholes do not allow individuals to become corporations and somehow access money in a way other than a salary, capital gain, or dividend. There are numerous details that would have to be gotten straight to make this a viable policy.

I am unsure of what the top marginal income tax rate would need to be in order to offset the ending of the corporate income tax and reinstating a federal inheritance tax as noted. The setting of this rate would require forecasting beyond my capabilities, but given that the corporate income tax has produced no more than 10% of federal revenue for the past 30 years, the top marginal rate should still be lower than it is currently (35%).

Inheritance Tax

Some reasonable inheritance tax should also be reinstated. The Fiscal Commission suggested using the 2009 federal inheritance tax structure that exempted the first $3.5 million in assets from the tax, with amounts above this having a tax of 45% applied to amounts above this, with a common sense updating for inflation. This seems a reasonable way forward.

Other Tax Changes I Have Proposed

As noted in Chap. 8, I favor lifting the wage cap to which the OASDI payroll tax applies, and recalibrating it to the 90th percentile. I think that the pace at which the Fiscal Commission calls for the phase in of this increase (fully linked to the 90th percentile by 2050) is too slow. I would favor moving more quickly to increase this payroll tax and essentially reestablishing the 1983 political deal for Social Security that has simply eroded due to the fact that wages in the top 10% of earners have risen much faster than have average wages.

I suggest the creation of a health care cost inflation payroll tax that would be triggered if long-term federal health care growth rates are not held to GDP growth plus 1 percentage point, and efforts by Congress to slow them do not work, or are not tried. This tax would be paid by employees only who were in the top half of the wage earners; I suggest 0.5% of payroll from the median wage on up, paid by workers only. I believe such a tax is needed because of the evidence that Americans have a far more difficult time making tradeoffs in the realm of health care as compared to other spheres. As noted in the previous chapter, study participants who were provided with accurate budget information did a fairly good job reducing the deficit that results from the discretionary portion of the budget as well as with Social Security. When it came to health care, however, they had a far more difficult time with Medicare. Further, the gestalt of the health care chapters (3–7) shows that there seems to be a persistent cultural inability to deal with limits in medicine and to practically address health care cost inflation and adopt methods to address the same.

This tax acknowledges that on the road to a sustainable health care system, we may decide that we really don't want to cut health care spending as much as we claim to want in the abstract. If so, the tax also provides us with a straightforward manner of paying for this decision.

Chapter 12
What Will It Take for Us to Act?

The basic policy details of this book are unchanged since I published the first edition in August 2011 because the problems facing our country are unchanged. In policy terms, we need to:

Enact policies that encourage economic growth in the short run
Adopt a long-range plan to move toward a sustainable budget

What has changed is that we are now in the midst of a Presidential election year. The payroll tax cut extension, agreed upon in February 2012, is likely to be the last consequential policy debate that results in any action prior to the 2012 election.

While it is unclear what short-term measures would be most effective at encouraging economic growth, "paying for" policies that have a goal of stimulating the economy (such as the extending the payroll tax cut through the remainder of 2012) with offsetting immediate cuts or making cuts in discretionary spending make little sense given the very low interest rate at which the US government can borrow money. This is akin to filling up a cup with a hole in the bottom.

The economy had an annualized growth rate of 1.1% in 2011, helped by short-term policies such as the payroll tax cut, but the reduction in government jobs and cuts in discretionary spending had a downward impact on GDP growth of around 0.5%. That simply means that economic growth would have been higher and unemployment lower if governments hadn't shed jobs and reduced other short-term spending last year.

There is a palpable sense for many that we have an unsustainable system and must do something, and I very much share this sentiment. However, the correct response has little to do with cutting current discretionary spending; we need a credible long-range plan to achieve a balanced budget, and this book has provided the why and how I would achieve this. Agreeing to one will be politically difficult because it will require conservatives to abandon pledges to never raise taxes, and progressives will have to focus attention on reform of programs such as Medicare and Social Security that are key priorities for us. If we ever have a balanced budget again, it will require an increase in taxes collected as a percent of GDP, and a reduction in planned spending as a percent of GDP, given the default. There is no easy way out.

Most importantly, a plan to move ahead on health reform is required if we are to ever have anything near a balanced budget again, simply because the spending side growth problem under the default scenario is primarily one of health care cost inflation. Health reform is the hardest step politically as well as technically, because it will require continued reform, will result in mistakes and disappointments, and require many course corrections. The default assumption should be that nothing will work to control costs given our past, but we have no choice but to try.

The main question is whether there is a policy consensus that can become a political deal to address these issues without our first suffering an economic calamity? It seems exceedingly unlikely that a Grand Bargain can be agreed to before the 2012 election short of some grave crisis, but the discussion of what such a plan should look like will remain a central 2012 campaign issue and beyond, especially in a virtually inevitable lame duck session of the 112th Congress that will have to determine whether to let major tax changes occur by default on January 1, 2013, or to replace them with some type of deal.

Politics of the Past Year

I believe the President made an error in not embracing the Fiscal Commission recommendations. I do not necessarily think that his embrace would have led to the needed Grand Bargain last year. In fact, since he has been elected, the President being for anything has seemed to ensure vehement Republican opposition. However, if he had embraced this proposal and put large portions of it in his budget last year (the tax reform proposal, for example), it could have (slightly) improved the chances of reaching a badly needed consensus deal to develop a sustainable budget. Further, it would have allowed the President and progressives to claim the mantle of truth tellers on our long-range budget issues, possibly providing some short-term political benefits with moderates and independents, but most importantly in beginning to educate Progressives that major changes are needed to achieve a sustainable budget, and that key progressive programs are put at risk if we delay and do not drive the changes.

Progressives undoubtedly reaped short-term political benefits by letting Republicans "go first": namely the unpopularity of the Medicare reform proposal that Paul Ryan included in his April 2011 budget proposal, which he has already seen fit to move away from. I am sure this vote will be successfully used against Republican candidates in the 2012 election, as it was in special elections in 2011, but our budget remains unsustainable and programs that are key for progressives will someday be reformed.

I believe there have been both short-term political and policy costs to progressives as well. In the political realm, not embracing the Fiscal Commission recommendations allowed Republicans to get away with talking about the fiscal problems of the nation in general terms while only tangibly engaging in small discretionary spending cuts that play well with their political base. This did nothing to solve our long-range problem and likely made the short run economy worse. And for all the bluster of the Medicare proposal contained in Paul Ryan's April 2011 budget, the hard legislative work of producing the fine print details that would have to be taken up by the House Ways and Means and Commerce Committees was never even begun.

By not embracing the Fiscal Commission recommendations, Progressives made it easier for Republicans to claim they wanted a balanced budget while still saying they would not raise taxes, while having no coherent health reform strategy (a plan and commitment to push it) beyond what they were against.

Finally, it is possible that going first and embracing the Fiscal Commission in his budget could have allowed the President to more forcefully argue for more short-term economic stimulus that was not "paid for" with offsetting cuts, because we would be moving toward a plan for a long-range sustainable budget. The opposition of Republicans to such stimulus measures, and the insistence of paying for others in the name of "addressing the budget deficit" would have been rendered far more hollow had Progressives been consistently embracing the Fiscal Commission plan that assumed an increase in taxes, implementing the ACA, and moving on to the next health reform steps. It would have been harder, and more politically costly for Republicans to have maintained their opposition to short-term economic measures and for the insistence at rendering the self-inflicted wound to our economy that was the debt ceiling debate and subsequent short-term deal to raise the debt ceiling limit.

Policy Consensus of the Past Year

In spite of both political parties essentially waiting for the other to go first with a serious proposal to develop a plan for a sustainable budget, there has been a quiet consensus reached about the structure that such a plan will take. There are similarities across a variety of large scale plans that have had some bipartisan discussion and support (Fiscal Commission, Domenici–Rivlin, Bipartisan Policy Center, Gang of 6 proposal in the Senate). Simply put, taxes must increase and spending must decrease over planned levels, and a major health reform effort must be at the heart of the policy to address the spending side.

In this sense, there are centrist plans to achieve a balanced budget that are plausible, and even more liberal ones that will work, such as the Center for American Progresses vision that would aim for balance at nearly 24% of GDP in around 25 years. While this level of expenditure is higher than what the "big plan consensus" that has emerged has settled on, it is far more plausible than any of the Republican alternatives put forth, because the Center for American Progress is willing to raise taxes substantially to achieve balance.

Republican plans are far less plausible because they have no health reform strategy that would enable us to achieve balance anywhere between 18 and 20% of GDP, which would require a profound slowing of health care cost inflation. In fact, they really have no health reform strategy at all, other than calling for repeal of the ACA. This means they have no credible strategy that could allow us to get federal spending anywhere near 18–19% of GDP given their affinity to continued large Defense spending.

Big Events in 2012

There are three major events that will take place during 2012 that will greatly impact the debate around developing a long-range sustainable budget: the Supreme Court's ruling on the constitutionality of the individual mandate in the ACA, the 2012 election, and the automatic reversion of the tax code to 2000 levels on January 1, 2013 in the absence of further action. A brief outline of how these events may play out follows (with emphasis on may!).

The Supreme Court should render its judgment regarding the constitutionality of the individual mandate and the Medicaid expansions that are central to the ACA at the end of its term in June 2012, just as the election season heats toward full boil. I don't know what they will decide, and will just handicap the politics and policy of what they might do.

It seems as though the short-term political risk of an adverse decision is greater for the Obama Administration than it is for Republicans so far as the 2012 election goes. If the law is struck down completely, then it will be a political blow to supporters of the ACA, and will remove a major accomplishment of the President. If the law is upheld, it would represent a victory for the President, but it will not decrease the rage of his political opponents and those who are opposed to the law, though perhaps some fence sitters will want to move on to implementation.

In policy terms, the ACA could be tweaked if the individual mandate is struck down but other aspects of the law allowed to go forward. For example, the soft individual mandates contained in Rep. Paul Ryan's Patients' Choice Act would be one route, or a move toward universal catastrophic insurance such as I have suggested would render the individual mandate moot. However, all such tweaks would require passage of new legislation, and that most certainly would not occur in the midst of a Presidential election.

The fate of the law will be determined by the 2012 election. If there is divided government after the 2012 election, and the Supreme Court upholds the mandate, then the ACA will not be repealed, and some sort of compromise way forward will need to be realized if we are to move toward a sustainable budget. However, if Republicans managed a clean sweep (President and both houses of Congress), then a full repeal is possible, but there is no reason to expect a replacement plan coming from Republican control of Washington. And without a robust health reform plan, there is no hope of a balanced budget, ever. In this sense, Republicans need a health reform deal far more than do the Democrats, because it is nearly impossible to imagine the Republicans mustering the political support necessary to pass a health reform plan, while Democrats have innumerable variations on reform in their back pockets.

The most predictably consequential event of the next year is the reversion of the income tax rates to pre-2001 levels and the payroll tax to 2010 levels on January 1, 2013. As many have noted, simply allowing all of the tax code to revert to the level the last time there was balanced budget would greatly reduce the deficit over the next 10 years, more so than even most deficit reduction plans. However, it would be better to more fully overhaul the tax code because it is outdated, but that logic so far has not led to a deal that would bring about a large scale tax reform that increases the amount of tax collected as a percent of GDP while seeking to make the code more conducive to economic growth. In short, there has to be a net tax increase, not a net tax cut if we are ever to have a balanced budget again.

If President Obama wins reelection, then an obvious strategy is to allow the tax code to revert on January 1, 2013 to prior levels, both the payroll tax as well as income tax rates, and to insist that the scheduled cuts as specified by the August 2011 deal to raise the debt ceiling be allowed to occur. From that point, a negotiation would begin to presumably undertake a tax reform that is similar to that proposed by the Fiscal Commission in which deductions and credits are reduced and rates lowered while increasing the amount of tax as a percent of GDP that is collected. This is necessary if we are to move toward a plan that can produce a long-range balanced budget.

If President Obama loses the election, then the most likely outcome seems to be an extension of the income tax rates for some period into the future, with a very unclear outcome for the payroll tax. Once the OASDI payroll tax has been 4.2% for 2 years, it will be very difficult to simply raise it back to 6.2% absent a large scale deal. In fact, the payroll tax cut for 2012 has likely upped the stakes for Progressives for the 2012 election, because if Republicans manage to take the White House and Senate while retaining the House of Representatives, then the issue of the payroll tax would likely provide Republicans with a great deal of leverage to bring about changes to Social Security that may not be to the liking of Progressives.

Hold Hands and Jump

The last three elections have essentially been won by one party making the case that they were not as bad as the "other side" and both Democrats and Republicans can see the route to 2012 election victories using their tried and true lines of attack intact. They want to raise taxes! They want to reduce Medicare spending!

In fact, we need to do both, in the long run, or we have no hope of a balanced budget.

I am a little league football coach, and one thing I try to focus on with the kids is that until the season is over, there is always an opportunity to redeem yourself, to bounce back with a better practice, to have a better game. And I think the same holds true for President Obama, and the Republicans.

There is an abiding sense that the last step of the "grand bargain" that will finally put us on the path to a sustainable budget is known, and that it looks a great deal like the plan put forth by the Fiscal Commission. I provided modifications in this book and endorse more robust health reforms than they did, and I think I am correct, but I would take the Fiscal Commission proposal lock, stock, and barrel in one second over the default of doing nothing.

What it will take for us to finally agree to a plan that will put us on the path to fiscal sustainability is for members of all political sides to swallow things they don't like for the good of the country, to hold hands and jump off the cliff together by agreeing to a "Grand Bargain." The system is set up against many small efforts to take on a problem so large, and we need to act. That doesn't mean there will not be tweaks and course corrections, especially in health reform, but we do need a big step, taken all together.

We will do it some day. The only question is whether we can muster the political courage to do it before an economic calamity leaves us with no choice and fewer options.